SUCH GREAT *recipes*

EVELYN HOEFAKKER

LifeRich Publishing is a registered trademark of The Reader's Digest Association, Inc.

LifeRich Publishing books may be ordered through booksellers or by contacting:

LifeRich Publishing
1663 Liberty Drive
Bloomington, IN 47403
www.liferichpublishing.com
1 (888) 238-8637

ISBN: 978-1-4897-0328-6 (sc)
ISBN: 978-1-4897-0329-3 (hc)
ISBN: 978-1-4897-0327-9 (e)

Library of Congress Control Number: 2014920075

Printed in the United States of America.

LifeRich Publishing rev. date: 1/23/2015

Introduction

As far back as I can remember, I've loved cooking, baking and eating the final result.

Even though we dined quite simply when I was a child, I remember enjoying special evenings when the table was set beautifully with delicious choices of food. Then there were those wonderful days spent at Oma and Opa's house. With fascination I would watch Oma make her perfect gravy that she served with her tasty pork chops and potatoes.

Later, when most teenagers were probably reading novels, I joined a cookbook club. It was a good day when a cookbook arrived in the mail for me! As my collection grew, so did my interest in food and cooking.

Since my first passion is food and the second one being eating it, it was in my best interests to build my life and career around it.

Landing a job at a newly opened restaurant just after high school spiked my love for pleasing people with food. That's what it's all about; making people happy with food! The display of the food, the aroma of it and especially the taste of it.

The recipes in this book were created to accommodate busy schedules, special events and for one hour cooking classes. And since a lot of them were first written for my students, they are written out with plenty of details. Not because they are complicated, but because I want everyone to achieve good results. If one of these recipes is the first one you tackle, I want it to turn out perfectly for you. Most of these recipes can be put together with ingredients that are readily available.

Having this cookbook in your hand, you'll want to know my credentials. I attended the Culinary School of Life, graduated from the School of the Love of Cooking and completed classes at the Institute of Appetites to Fill. There are actually no letters behind my name unless you count Mom, wife, friend, caterer or cooking teacher!

Now, since I started with this whole cookbook idea, a lot of things had to give. My family has been very accommodating as the office became a storage room for cooking equipment and dishes, the living room a photo studio and the kitchen mostly a mess. It has not been uncommon to stop everything to do photos for the blog or for the cookbook. Mostly, though, we have had a lot of fun and some pretty good meals!

Use this book of great recipes to make memories with your family and friends. Use the photos to tempt yourself into trying the recipes. Most of all, enjoy serving people food and happiness.

Contents

Great Beginnings- Appetizers and Salads

The Soup Ladle

Dinners

The Accompaniments-Potatoes, Rice, Vegetables and Sauces

Muffins and Quick Breads

Sweet Endings, Sweet Beginnings and Some Sweet Beverages

Great Beginnings~
Appetizers and Salads

This collection of amazing appetizers and salads have been copied several times over the years both for my children to make and for the cooking class students to prepare. Most likely there will be many of these that you will end up sharing as well!

Smoked Salmon Bruschetta

Makes: about 15 slices

It was declared that **Smoked Salmon Bruschetta** was "amazing" and that I must share the recipe! This Bruschetta *is* really good, both heated or chilled. Chives are added to the filling because they grow so well around here, but green onions are good too.

1 baguette loaf, unsliced so you can slice it diagonally
2 to 3 tbsp. butter, softened
8 oz. smoked salmon
4 oz. soft cream cheese
3 tbsp. mayonnaise

1 tsp dried parsley flakes
½ tsp dill
⅛ tsp black pepper
2 tbsp. finely chopped chives (or green onions)
½ cup shredded Monterey Jack cheese

Method:

- Preheat oven to 450° F. Cover a baking sheet with parchment paper or use non-stick cooking spray to coat the baking sheet.
- Slice the baguette loaf on an angle in ¾ inch slices.
- Lightly butter them on both sides.
- Toast them for about 8 minutes or until they are golden brown. Set the toasted slices aside while you prepare the topping.*
- Turn the oven down to 350° F.
- In a medium size bowl, mix the smoked salmon with the cream cheese, mayo and seasonings until it is combined well but not smooth, so you can see the salmon chunks.
- Top the toasted baguette slices with about 1 ½ tbsp. of the salmon topping.
- Place a little shredded cheese on top of the salmon. The toasts may be served cold without the addition of cheese at this point.
- Bake the Smoked Salmon Bruschetta for about 10 minutes more or until the cheese is melted.

Total prep and bake time: 1 hour
*Toasts and the salmon topping may be made a couple days ahead.

Note: *Tie the ends of a small bunch of chives to create a beautiful chive garnish.*

Notes & Quotes

Jalapeno Cheese Bread
Makes: about 14 slices

I've had so many requests for this cheese bread! We have made it numerous times in cooking classes but also for several events. It usually is one of the items on the buffet that is hard to keep stocked. This bread makes a wonderful appetizer, but it is also great with dinner.

1 loaf French bread sliced lengthwise
3 cups shredded mozzarella cheese
¾ cup mayonnaise
¾ cup very soft butter

2 tbsp. Parmesan cheese
1 jalapeno, chopped
½ cup sliced green onions, optional

Method:

- Preheat oven to 350° F. Line a cookie sheet with foil and spray it with non-stick cooking spray.
- Shred the cheese onto piece of wax paper. (this just makes it easier to shred and easier to pick up)
- In a medium size bowl, combine the butter, mayonnaise, Parmesan, jalapenos and the sliced green onions. Stir in the shredded cheese. This can be done with a wooden spoon.
- Spread the cheesy topping onto the bread halves all the way to edges, nice and thick!
- Place the bread on the prepared cookie sheet and bake for 15 to 20 minutes until it is nice and golden around the edges and the cheese is melted.
- Let the baked bread rest for 5 minutes before using a pizza cutter to cut it into diagonal slices to serve.

Total prep and bake time: about 35 minutes

Note: *What I really like about this bread is that it can be made a few days ahead, wrapped and then baked when you need it.*

Greek Sliders
Makes: 10 to 12 Sliders

The flavors of Greece!
These are amazing! They are juicy, tangy and deliciously beefy. We like them served with extra sides of Feta cheese and Tzatziki Sauce. Isn't anything mini just more fun?

1 recipe Tzatziki sauce (page 15)
12 small slider rolls (I like the "semi-homemade" Rhodes rolls)
Lettuce topping:
8 leaves Romaine lettuce
Juice of ½ lemon
1 tbsp. olive oil
Salt and pepper to taste
Mini Beef Patties:
1 pound lean ground beef

2 tbsp. dry bread crumbs
1 egg
1 tbsp. Greek salad dressing
1 to 2 tbsp. crumbled Feta cheese
½ tsp oregano
¼ tsp pepper
½ tsp salt
Additional Ingredients:
Feta cheese and Tzatziki sauce

Method:

- Prepare the Tzatziki sauce and bake the rolls if you have decided to do the "home-made" version.
- Slice the Romaine lettuce into half-inch strips and then chop them again to make about 2 inch sized strips.
- Toss the Romaine in a medium bowl with the lemon juice, olive oil and the salt and pepper. You may add Feta cheese to the salad if you like.
- Prepare the beef patties by combining all the patty ingredients in another bowl. Do not over mix the beef with the other ingredients as this will make them tough. Form the beef into about 12-two inch patties or to fit your rolls.
- Fry or grill the slider patties for about 5 minutes on each side or until the juices run clear. (We preferred them fried rather than grilled.)
- To assemble the wonderful Greek Sliders, spread plenty of Tzatziki sauce on both sides of the bun and top with a little Feta cheese.
- Place the beef patty on the bottom of the bun and top it with some Feta cheese and then the Romaine salad.
- Secure the Greek Sliders with a toothpick* and place them on a Greek serving platter with extra sauce and Feta cheese.

Total prep and cooking time: 45 minutes to 1 hour
* They have a tendency to *slide* apart, so a toothpick helps avoid that.

Note: *Turn this into dinner by serving 2 of these to each guest and adding the* **Greek Fresh Vegetable Salad.** *(recipe page 16)*

Notes & Quotes

Spinach and Artichoke Dip with Pimentos
Yield: about 10 servings

Spinach and Artichoke Dip with Pimentos has a little "kick" to it. The pimentos add color and give it even more interesting flavor. Pita chips, tortilla chips or toasted baguette slices work well for scooping up this satisfying dip. It can be baked in an 8 x 8 dish or baked in small individual servings. If you find yourself eating this with a spoon to get every last bit out of the dish, don't feel bad, it happens all the time! Make sure you use fresh shredded Parmesan cheese in this recipe.

⅓ cup butter
½ cup chopped onions
1 large garlic clove, minced
6 tbsp. flour
1 cup half and half
½ cup milk
4 oz. cream cheese, cut into chunks
1 ½ tbsp. fresh squeezed lemon juice

¼ to ½ tsp salt
⅛ tsp pepper
⅛ tsp cayenne (more or less to taste)
10 oz. cooked, drained and chopped spinach*
1-15 oz. can artichoke hearts, drained and chopped coarsely
3 tbsp. diced pimentos
1 ½ cups shredded Parmesan, divided

Method:

- Preheat the oven to 400° F. Prepare an 8x8 baking dish or 8 individual baking dishes, by coating them with non-stick cooking spray.
- Cook the chopped onion in the butter until the onion is tender. Add the garlic and cook it for one more minute.
- Sprinkle the flour over the cooking onions and garlic. Stir it until the flour is bubbling a little.
- Slowly whisk in the cream and the milk to make a thick sauce.
- When the sauce comes to a boil, stir in the cream cheese until the sauce is smooth.
- Remove the sauce from the heat and add the remaining ingredients, except just use half of the shredded Parmesan.
- Spoon the Spinach and Artichoke Dip with Pimentos into the prepared dish or dishes. It may be chilled to reheat later in the day at this point.
- Top the dip with the remaining shredded Parmesan cheese.
- Bake uncovered for 20 to 25 minutes for the full dish and about 10 to 15 minutes for the individual dishes. The cheese should be melted and golden.

Total prep and baking time: about 50 minutes

Notes & Quotes

*I prefer to use spinach that I have cooked from fresh. I cook it just until it wilts and then drain and chop it. This gives the whole dish more spinach flavor.

Chicken Croquettes

Makes: 16 Croquettes

On New Year's Eve my family always celebrates with plenty of appetizers and beverages. Since we are of Dutch heritage there are some traditional foods that we enjoy. Croquettes are one of those specialties.

Vegetable oil for frying
3 tbsp. butter
1 tbsp. finely chopped onions
1 tbsp. finely chopped celery
4 tbsp. flour
¾ cups chicken stock
¼ cup cream
1 tbsp. parsley flakes
1 tsp salt

¼ tsp pepper
1 to 2 tsp curry powder
1 tbsp. Worcestershire sauce
2 cups cooked and shredded chicken
1 cup shredded Gouda or Swiss cheese
Egg dip Coating:
2 eggs whisked together with 2 tbsp. water
Bread Crumb Coating:
2 cups dry bread crumbs

Method:

- Pour about 3 inches of oil into a medium size cooking pot.
- In a medium size saucepan, cook the onion and celery in the butter until it is tender.
- Sprinkle the flour over the cooked celery and onions and cook it slightly.
- Slowly whisk in the chicken stock to make a thick sauce.
- Stir in the seasonings and the chicken and cook it for about 1 more minute.
- Remove it from the heat and stir in the cheese.
- Place the cooked filling on a plate to chill in the freezer until it is cool enough to handle.
- Meanwhile prepare the crumbs and the egg dip. Start heating the oil on the stove.
- When the filling is cool enough to handle, form it into rolls that are about 1 by 2 inches.
- Lightly roll them in them in the egg mixture and then coat them in the crumbs. Do this twice with each croquette.
- Place the croquettes in the freezer to firm them up slightly. (They may be frozen for a later use at this point if you like.)
- Carefully drop the croquettes in the hot oil, cooking about 5 at a time.
- Flip the croquette over when the side is golden, about 6 minute's total.
- Use a slotted spoon to remove them and place them on a paper towel to absorb some of the grease.
- Serve with Dijon mustard when they are still hot.

Total prep and cooking time: about 1 hour

Note: *These also may be shaped into 1 inch balls.*

Notes & Quotes

Parmesan and Herb Breadsticks

Makes: 16 to 20 Breadsticks

Sometimes after spending hours in the kitchen making an elaborate meal, the one thing I hear the most raves about is the bread or rolls! And, although I'm pretty sure they enjoyed everything else, there is just something amazing about good bread! Someone once told me that if everything else is terrible, and the dinner rolls are awesome, that's all your guests will remember. While I wouldn't go *that* far, I do believe they complete the meal.

Parmesan and Herb Bread Sticks are great with a meal or as an appetizer. These are simple to make with purchased bread dough, but if you want to make your own bread dough that works great too. The dough should not be cold as that makes it hard to roll out. Including the "rise time", these bread sticks will be ready to eat in about an hour, providing the dough is at room temperature when you start.

1 loaf thawed to room temperature, previously frozen bread dough
¾ cup melted butter
1 ½ cups Parmesan cheese
2 tsp garlic powder

2 tsp dried parsley flakes
½ tsp dried oregano
½ tsp dried basil
¼ tsp salt
⅛ tsp black pepper

Method:

- Prepare a baking sheet by spraying it with non-stick cooking spray.
- Roll out the dough to ½ inch thickness. Slice into strips {about 16-20 strips} using a pizza cutter.
- Combine the Parmesan cheese with the seasonings in a shallow bowl. Place the melted butter in a shallow bowl as well.
- Dip the bread sticks in the butter to completely coat them.
- Roll the buttered stick in the herb and Parmesan cheese bowl.
- Place them on the prepared baking sheet about 2 inches apart.
- Set the tray aside for about 25 minutes to let them rise a little.
- Preheat oven to 350 degrees. Bake the bread sticks for about 15 minutes or until golden.
- Serve warm Parmesan bread sticks with Marinara sauce (recipe page 64) as an appetizer or serve them with your dinner.

Total prep, rising and bake time: 1 hour

Notes & Quotes

Note: *Non-stick cooking spray is an amazing invention! Use it to ensure your clean-up is quick and easy.*

Mexican Tortilla Roll-ups

Makes: 36 roll-ups

8 small soft tortillas
8 to 12 slices deli roast beef
1 - 8 oz. package softened cream cheese
½ package taco seasoning mix

3 tbsp. diced green chili peppers, drained
1 cup cheddar cheese, shredded

Method:

- Dump the soft cream cheese into the mixing bowl.
- Add the taco seasoning and the chili peppers and mix with the wooden spoon. It is a little stiff at first but after a while it will become smooth.
- Spread a large spoonful onto each of the tortillas. Make sure you go all the way to the edges.
- Sprinkle each tortilla with a little bit of the cheese.
- Place a slice of roast beef onto each tortilla. If you need to, cut one slice in half to cover the tortilla.
- Roll up the tortilla nice and tight making sure the roast beef doesn't slide out.
- Slice the tortillas and place them on a serving platter.

Total prep time: 30 minutes

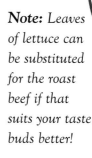

Note: *Leaves of lettuce can be substituted for the roast beef if that suits your taste buds better!*

Italian Salami Pinwheels

Makes: 20 pinwheels

4 small tortillas
2 tbsp. Basil pesto {recipe page 64}
4oz cream cheese

1 tbsp. mayonnaise
16 slices Italian Salami
12 slices Monterey Jack cheese

Method:

- Use a small bowl to combine the basil pesto with the cream cheese. Beat with an electric mixer until smooth.
- Add the mayonnaise and stir until smooth. This creamy spread may be chilled for later use at this point.
- Spread the sauce onto the tortillas all the way to the edges. You will be using about 2 tbsp. on each tortilla.
- Layer the salami and cheese over the pesto spread. Roll the tortilla up very tight. They may be chilled for up to 3 days at this point.
- Slice the tortillas into ⅓ inch slices. Serve or chill. Total prep time: about 30 minutes

Note: *The Creamy Basil Pesto Spread is wonderful with tortilla chips!*

Fruit Platter Success!

There are a few simple steps to a beautiful Fresh Fruit Platter. After working with slippery melons, wet grapes, and dull knives I have learned a few things.

- Always pick out the best looking fruit and wash and dry it well.
- Use a very sharp knife and a large cutting board.
- Tuck fresh kale leaves around the edge of the tray before you place the sliced fruit.
- Lay the fruit on the side that will best stay in place and hold the fruit tight as you slice it. Fruit that is trimmed of its peels displays best.
- Slice the fruit in even sized pieces and hold the stack together the best you can as you place it on the tray.
- Place grape bunches and strawberries in the spaces between the rows and use them to keep the rows even.
- Tuck extra kale leaves in the spaces that need filler or more color.
- Pat any juices dry with clean paper towel to keep all the fruit from sliding together.
- Cover the platter well with plastic wrap and chill it until you are ready to set it out.

Bacon and Tomato Spread

Makes: 1 ½ cups spread

1 cup sour cream
½ cup crumbled bacon
¼ cup peeled, seeded and chopped tomato
½ cup grated cheddar cheese

1 tsp Ranch seasoning mix
1 tsp Worcestershire sauce
1 tbsp. diced green onions or chives
Hot Pepper sauce-a few shakes

Method:

- Fry and then chop the cooked bacon. (Fresh bacon is best but you may use real bacon bits.)
- Combine all the ingredients in a medium size bowl, stirring gently to combine. The spread may be served right away but the flavors improve if it is chilled for at least an hour.
- Place the spread in a serving bowl with a spoon or a spreader on a platter with assorted crackers.
- Bacon and Tomato Spread will keep for about 3 days in the refrigerator. Prep time: 20 minutes.

Guacamole

Makes: 1 cup

Dipping your favorite crispy snack into this creamy and healthy Guacamole is the best thing! Guacamole is not difficult to make, it is just difficult to keep fresh. By using a zip lock bag to mash the ingredients together, you keep the avocados green and fresh.

2 ripe avocados
½ tbsp. fresh squeezed lime juice
½ tsp salt
½ cup minced onion (red onions are nice)

½ small tomato, finely chopped
½ tsp garlic powder
⅛ tsp cayenne powder or more to taste

Method:

- Place all ingredients listed into a heavy duty zip lock bag, zipped securely.
- Squish, squeeze and mash all those wonderful ingredients together until it is good and smooth.
- Chill the bag of Guacamole until you are ready to serve it.
- Snip the edge off the bag to squeeze it out into a bowl. Stir it slightly.
- Garnish it with a few flakes of hot pepper to warn folks about the heat!

Fresh Herb Dip and Spread

Makes: approx. 1 ¼ cups spread or 1 ½ cups dip

Complete your party table with this fresh and tasty spread. Beat in some smoked salmon and pipe it into Phyllo pastry cups, or pipe it into scooped out cucumber rounds to make Cucumber Canapés.

4 oz. cream cheese
¼ cup sour cream
¼ cup mayonnaise
1 tbsp. vinegar
¼ cup fresh chopped parsley

1 tbsp. fresh dill, chopped fine
⅛ tsp black pepper
½ tsp salt
½ tsp garlic powder

Method:

- With an electric mixer, beat the cream cheese until smooth. Add the sour cream and then the mayonnaise while beating.
- Gently stir in the remaining ingredients.
- Stir in any additional ingredients* as desired.
- Chill spread for about an hour before serving to enhance the flavors.
- This spread can be used to top crackers or cucumber canapés. Some extra toppings can be set on your platter such as shrimp, avocado, smoked salmon, or olives.
- To make this recipe into a **dip** for vegetables whisk in: ¼ cup milk

Total prep time: about 15 minutes
*Additional ingredient suggestions: smoked salmon, sun dried tomatoes, chopped Pepperoncini, chives, or cheese etc. Dried seasonings may be used to replace the fresh ones, just use a third less.

Note: *On the photo on page one you can see the Smoked Salmon Filling in Phyllo cups.*

Notes & Quotes

Tzatziki Sauce

Makes: about 4 cups or 12 servings

This sauce is essential for the Greek Sliders and the Gyros. It just may be the healthiest and tastiest sauce there ever was! Go ahead and eat this right out of the dish.

2 cups Greek plain yogurt or plain yogurt
2 cups very finely chopped cucumber (1 small cucumber)
3 tbsp. fresh squeezed lemon juice
2 tbsp. mayonnaise

½ tsp garlic powder
¼ tsp black pepper
¼ tsp dried dill
½ tsp salt

Method:

- Peel and chop the cucumber into very small pieces. Place it in a strainer to remove some of the juices.
- Add the chopped cucumber to the yogurt, lemon juice and the remaining ingredients. Use a medium size bowl.
- Stir well and chill until ready to use. Stir before using. This sauce benefits from chilling for at least an hour.

Total prep time: 15 minutes

Creamy Chicken con Queso

Yield: serves 8 to 10

My students love to share this with other students and always receive many compliments for it! Creamy Chicken con Queso can be served as a dip for Tortilla chips but it also work well scooped into a soft tortilla with perhaps some lettuce and tomato.

2 cups cooked diced chicken
1 can cream of chicken soup
½ cup sour cream
½ cup prepared salsa

½ cup shredded cheddar cheese
⅛ tsp Tabasco sauce (or more to taste)
Topping:
½ cup shredded Colby Jack cheese

Method:

- Preheat oven to 375° F. Prepare an 8x8 square pan by coating it with non-stick cooking spray.
- In a medium size bowl stir together all the ingredients except for the cheese topping.
- Scoop the creamy mixture into the prepared 8x8 dish. Cover the dish with tin foil.
- Bake for 20 to 25 minutes or until it is bubbling around the edges.
- Remove the Creamy Chicken con Queso from the oven and top it with the shredded Colby Jack cheese.
- It may be served immediately after the cheese is melted.

Total prep and baking time: 40 minutes

Greek Fresh Vegetable Salad with White Beans

Serves: 8

This salad gets eaten in stages at our house. Some of my daughters just eat the cucumbers, one of them picks out the olives, I pick out the onions, my son pushes the beans aside and my husband eats it all! Oh, and I use a spoon to finish off any remaining dressing!

1 long English cucumber
2 Roma tomatoes
¼ cup chopped red onion
1 green pepper
1 cup black olives or Kalamata olives
½ cup to 1 cup crumbled Feta cheese
1-15 oz can drained white beans

Dressing:
½ cup bottled Greek dressing
½ cup olive oil
2 tbsp. fresh squeezed lemon juice
1 tbsp. vinegar
1 ½ tsp crumbled oregano
⅛ to ¼ tsp salt (to taste)
⅛ tsp pepper
½ tsp garlic powder

Method:

- Peel and chop the cucumber into ½ inch size pieces.
- Chop the green peppers, onions and tomatoes in about ½ inch size pieces as well.
- Place all the vegetables, olives and the Feta cheese in a large bowl.
- Whisk together the dressing ingredients and taste to see if it has the *zip* you are after.
- Pour the dressing over the vegetables to coat them well.
- Add the drained beans and stir everything carefully as to not crush or break the beans.
- Transfer the **Fresh Greek Salad** to a serving bowl and let it chill for a couple hours or the whole day. This may be served immediately but chilling it enhances the flavor.
- Gently stir the salad before serving and garnish it with additional Feta cheese and oregano.

Total prep time: about ½ hour

Note: *White beans may be eliminated to result in a wonderful Fresh Greek Salad.*

Notes & Quotes

Mediterranean Pasta Salad

Serves: about 12

Abundant color and flavor make this pasta salad incredibly popular. Of all salads
that I make, I probably make this one the most often. It may be made and served
on the same day but preparing it the day before gives it the most flavor.

1 12 oz. box tri colored Rotini
½ red pepper, diced
½ green pepper, diced
2 tbsp. finely sliced carrot pieces
¼ cup diced red onion
3 oz. sliced or whole black olives
1 tbsp. dried parsley flakes

1 ½ cups prepared Italian dressing, divided
1 tbsp. vinegar
½ tsp garlic powder
½ tsp dried oregano, crumbled
Salt and pepper to taste
1 long English cucumber, peeled and diced
2 Roma tomatoes, cut into cubes

Method:

- Cook Rotini according to package directions. Cool by running cold water over the noodles. Drain it and set it aside.
- Meanwhile, chop all the vegetables except for the cucumbers and tomatoes. Place them in medium size bowl.
- Add the Rotini, add 1 cup of the dressing and seasoning and toss together to completely coat the noodles. (To finish the salad immediately, add the remaining dressing, the cucumbers and tomatoes.)
- Chill the salad overnight for the best flavor. Stir it occasionally to make sure all the juices are absorbed into the noodles.
- Add the cucumber and tomatoes and the remaining Italian dressing (or more if needed) and chill for a few more hours.

Total prep time: about ½ hour

Notes & Quotes

Note: *This salad has gone on many vacations with us and everyone always raves about it!*

Favorite Coleslaw

Yield: serves 8

I just love a good coleslaw, and when experimenting with different dressings and sauces, I found this one to be the one with just the right amount of tangy, sweet and creamy and therefore it became a favorite.

10 cups shredded green cabbage
1 cup shredded red cabbage
1 cup shredded carrots
⅔ cup apple cider vinegar

⅔ cup white sugar
¼ to ⅓ cup mayonnaise
¼ tsp salt or to taste
⅛ tsp pepper or to taste

Method:

- Place the cabbages and the shredded carrots in a large bowl.
- Add the cider vinegar and the sugar to the cabbage and let it soak for about 30 minutes or more at room temperature. Toss it lightly to ensure everything is soaked.
- Drain the juices off of the slaw and stir in the mayonnaise and the salt and pepper.
- Serve the coleslaw soon after the addition of the mayonnaise.

Total prep and chill time: 1 hour

Marinated Vegetables

Yield: 6 servings

6 carrots, cut julienne style
3 celery sticks
1 each yellow and red pepper
Marinade:
4 tbsp. vegetable oil
6 tbsp. white wine vinegar

1 tbsp. sugar
½ tsp salt
¼ tsp pepper
¼ tsp garlic powder
½ tsp each basil, oregano and parsley flakes

Method:

- Chop the vegetables in strips that are equal in size and length.
- Place about 1 inch of water in a medium saucepan. Bring it to a boil.
- Add the vegetables to the boiling water and cook for just 5 minutes.
- Meanwhile, mix the marinade together in a medium size bowl.
- Drain the vegetables well and add them to the marinade. Toss the vegetables to coat them well. Chill the marinated vegetables until they are cold and stir them before serving.

Creamy Fruit Salad

Yield: 25 servings

Homemade fruit juice dressing really makes this salad! Using fresh *real* whipped cream and maybe some of your own canned fruit, sets this winter fruit salad above the rest. Or as in my case, my dear mother in laws' canned fruit! Thanks, Mom!

Dressing:
1 tbsp. cornstarch
2 tbsp. sugar
1 tbsp. lemon juice

½ cup pineapple juice (use juice drained off the pineapple)
1 egg yolk, lightly beaten

Method:

- Stir the cornstarch with the sugar in a small saucepan.
- Add the juices and stir well. Whisk in the egg yolk.
- Cook and stir over medium heat until mixture just comes to a boil. Remove from the heat.
- Cover the saucepan and chill it until it is firm and cold, about 2 hours or freeze it in a thin layer to speed up the process.

Note: Creamy Fruit Salad *is a great Thanksgiving dinner accompaniment. It can easily be made a day ahead and kept cold.*

Notes & Quotes

Meanwhile beat:

½ cup whipping cream
½ tsp vanilla

1 tbsp. powdered sugar

Method:

- Chill the whipped cream while the cooked juices are chilling. Whipped cream should be quite stiff.

Fruit:

1 - 20 oz. can pineapple tidbits, drained
1 - 15 oz. can diced peaches, drained (or cut up the sliced to get pieces)
1 - 15 oz. can diced pears, drained

1 - 15 oz. can mandarin orange segments, drained
2 cups red and green grapes, large ones sliced in half

Method:

- Place all the fruit in a strainer to drain all the juices out. Include the grapes as this prevents them from turning brown.
- Chill the drained fruit while you are waiting for the dressing to chill.
- Pat the fruit with paper towels to make sure no juices remain. Place fruit in a large bowl.

- Fold the whipped cream into the chilled fruit juice mixture. The chilled fruit juice mixture will be quite stiff. Start by adding a little beaten cream to it to make it easier to fold into the rest of the whipped cream.
- Fold all the fruit into the lovely creamy and fruity dressing.
- Place in a large beautiful serving bowl to show off your wonderful salad!
- Chill the salad until you are ready to serve it.

Total prep and cooking time: about 1 hour if you use the freezer to chill the dressing.

Cucumber and Tomato Salad

Serves 5

When the sun ripens the tomatoes and cucumbers to perfection, it is time to make this salad. It is important that I double or even triple this recipe in order to have a little left to bring to the dinner table for my family to enjoy!

2 long English cucumbers, peeled
2 medium size ripe tomatoes, cut up
2 tbsp. lemon juice
1 tbsp. vinegar

1 tbsp. vegetable oil
1 tbsp. sugar
¼ tsp salt
1/8 tsp pepper

Method:

- Slice the peeled cucumbers very thin using the large slicing side of a stand-up grater.
- Place the cucumbers in a medium size bowl.
- Cut up the tomatoes into ½ inch size chunks and add them to the cucumbers.
- Pour the lemon juice, vinegar, oil and the seasonings over the cucumber and tomatoes.
- Stir the salad well and let it rest for at least ten minutes before serving. Stir before serving this healthy and satisfying salad.

The Soup Ladle

If my family were to explain what comfort food was, I think soup would probably be the first food that would come to mind. Steaming soup being ladled into bowls on a chilly evening, is the ultimate in comfort. The soups in this chapter are thick and satisfying and are hearty enough to be served as a meal.

French Cream of Tomato Soup

Makes: 6 to 8 servings

Why French? Because *you* are a gourmet!
After serving this French Cream of Tomato Soup for a small luncheon, I wanted my daughters
to try it. Since they don't like tomatoes very much, I *kind of* forced them. After a few
spoonful's, they were asking for more! The remaining leftovers were "called" immediately.

¼ cup butter
¼ cup finely chopped onion
1 small garlic clove, minced
3 tbsp. flour
45 oz. canned diced tomatoes
1 ½ cups chicken broth
½ cup white wine

½ tsp salt
4 tsp sugar
⅛ to ¼ tsp pepper, (to taste)
½ cup half and half (light cream)
Garnish:
¼ cup heavy cream
1 tbsp parsley flakes

Method:

- Sauté the onions and garlic in the butter until they are barely tender. Make sure they are not brown.
- Sprinkle the flour over the cooking onions and stir until it thickens.
- Slowly stir in the canned tomatoes and cook and stir until the tomatoes and onions come to a low boil.
- Place the hot, cooked tomato mixture in a blender to make it completely smooth. (or use a hand held blender)
- Return the smooth mixture to the pan and add all the remaining ingredients except the cream. Bring the soup to a boil while stirring.
- After the soup has boiled, remove it from the heat and add the cream.
- Ladle the soup into bowls and carefully spoon about a tablespoon of heavy cream* into each bowl, just before serving. Garnish with parsley flakes.

Total prep and cook time: about 45 minutes

Notes & Quotes

Note: *The heavy cream adds both flavor and visual appeal to the French Cream of Tomato Soup.*

Chicken or Turkey Noodle Soup

Makes: 8 bowls

When you need a light dinner or a warm lunch, this chicken noodle soup is a great choice. Using leftover turkey or chicken makes this soup very quick and easy. From start to placing it on the table, this soup only takes about 45 minutes. You could even whip up some biscuits while it is cooking!

2 sticks celery, diced
1 small carrot, peeled and chopped fine
¼ cup chopped onions
¼ cup chopped red pepper
8 cups chicken broth or stock

½ tsp salt
¼ tsp pepper
1 tbsp. parsley flakes
1 ½ cups uncooked noodles
3 cups cooked and diced chicken or turkey

Method:

- In a large pot, bring the chicken stock, vegetables and the salt and pepper to a boil. Turn heat to low and simmer ten minutes or until vegetables are tender.
- Add the noodles and the parsley and cook for about 15 minutes more or until the noodles are cooked.
- Toss in the cooked chicken or turkey to heat it through. This should only take about 3 more minutes.
- Add additional salt and pepper to taste.
- Serve hot with rolls or biscuits. Pictured on the chapter title page.

Total prep and cooking time: 45 minutes

Notes & Quotes

Note: *After Thanksgiving we are quite often looking for a recipe to use up all that leftover turkey. You can dice up some of that turkey to use for this soup.*

Vegetable Beef Barley Soup
Makes: 8 meal sized servings

This is another one of those recipes that really dates me. I'm pretty sure I've been making it for almost twenty five years! I guess there will be no doubt that you can trust this soup to be good. It also freezes well.

1 pound lean ground beef
½ cup chopped onions
1 tsp seasoning salt
⅛ tsp pepper
2 large carrots
3 stalks celery
8 cups beef stock or more for thinner soup

1-15 oz. can petite diced tomatoes
3 tbsp. tomato paste
½ cup pearled barley
1 tsp dried basil
1 tbsp. dried parsley flakes
½ tsp seasoning salt
Pepper to taste

Method:

- Brown the ground beef in a large soup pot.
- Add the chopped onions, one teaspoon of the seasoning salt and the pepper while the beef is browning.
- Chop the celery and dice the carrots and add them to the soup pot.
- Pour the beef stock, the diced tomatoes and the tomato paste over the vegetables and bring the soup to a boil.
- When the soup is boiling, add the barley and the remaining seasonings.
- Cover the soup after it has returned to boiling and cook on low heat for about 1 hour or until the barley is tender.

Total prep and cooking time: 1 hour and 15 minutes

Notes & Quotes

Note: Soup is almost always better the next day so plan ahead!

Creamy Chicken and Wild Rice Soup

Yield: serves 8

Creamy Chicken and Wild Rice Soup is thick, full of vegetables and big on flavor! Add a few dinner rolls and it is hearty enough to be a meal in itself. We found that this soup is best served the day it is made. It is simple to make since it is thickened using a "slurry".

9 cups chicken broth
3 sticks of celery, chopped
½ cup chopped carrots
½ cup chopped red pepper
¼ cup chopped onions
1-9 oz. box Uncle Ben's Herbed Wild Rice Mix*

2 ½ cups chopped chicken, dark and white is fine
¼ to ½ tsp black pepper
1 tbsp. dried parsley flakes
Slurry:
¾ cup flour
2 cups half and half

Method:

- In a large soup pot cook the vegetables in the chicken broth.
- When the vegetables and stock come to a boil, add the wild rice mix without the seasoning.
- Stir the vegetables and rice together and return it to boiling.
- Add the chicken and the seasoning mix plus the additional seasonings. (parsley and pepper)
- Cover the soup and cook it for about 30 minutes or until the rice is tender.
- Make slurry with the flour and the half and half. (Simply whisk the cream briskly into the flour in a medium size bowl until it is very smooth.)
- While the soup is boiling and while you whisk the soup, pour in the slurry.
- Stir the soup constantly until it comes to a boil again and it is nice and thick.
- Remove the soup from the heat and serve immediately, garnished with a little fresh ground pepper, of course!

Total prep and cooking time: about 1 hour
* You can make your own rice and seasoning if you like. Use ¼ cup wild rice and ¾ cup converted rice and add some seasoning salt, herbs and pepper. Be sure to soak this wild rice a few hours first.

Notes & Quotes

"One cannot think well, love well, or sleep well if one has not dined well".

– *Virginia Wolf*

Quick Meatball Minestrone

Serves: 8

A little bit of Italy! Quick Meatball Minestrone only takes about 45 minutes from start to serving time if you have the meatballs ready to go. It has an amazing amount of flavor considering that it is only cooked for half an hour! The generous amount of vegetables and beans makes it a hearty and healthy dinner.

24 small pre-baked meatballs (use meatball recipe on page 36)
6 cups beef broth or water with 2 beef bouillon cubes
¼ cup chopped onions
1 garlic clove, minced
¾ cup *each* of chopped carrots, celery and green cabbage
1 –15 oz. can drained Great Northern beans or white beans

1 –15 oz. can petite diced tomatoes
1 large bay leaf
1 tsp dried basil, crushed*
¼ tsp pepper
½ tsp seasoning salt
1 cup pasta shells or any desired pasta choice
2 tbsp. chopped fresh parsley
¼ cup fresh grated Parmesan cheese

Method:

- In a 4 quart cooking pot combine the meatballs, broth, tomatoes, beans, all the vegetables and the seasonings.
- Bring the vegetables and seasoned broth to a boil.
- When the soup comes to a boil, add the pasta.
- Cover and simmer the Minestrone for about 20 minutes. Remove bay leaf.
- Stir in the fresh parsley and garnish each serving with Parmesan cheese.

Unused Quick Meatball Minestrone may be refrigerated for about 3 days. Reheat the soup on low heat.

Total prep and cooking time: 45 minutes

*To crush the basil, simply rub it in the palm of your hand using your thumb. This process just gives the basil more flavor.

Dinners

It is a good week when several of the dinners from this chapter are featured on our fridge's menu and reminder board!

Oven Baked Parmesan Chicken with Marinara Sauce

Yield: Serves 8

Parmesan Chicken with Marinara Sauce has *layers* of good flavors! There is the juicy chicken, the crispy coating, the zesty sauce and a finishing touch of Parmesan cheese! And easy to make too! The coating and the sauce can be prepared in advance to save time at cooking time. This chicken is a favorite at our house and even my skeptical little boy cleans his plate!

Chicken:
4 chicken breasts sliced into 8 pieces
Flour coating:
½ tsp salt
¼ pepper
½ cup flour
Dip into:
½ cup melted butter, or more as needed

Crumb Coating:
3 cups toasted fresh bread crumbs*
¾ cups Parmesan cheese
1 tsp garlic powder
¼ cup finely chopped fresh parsley or 1 tbsp. dried parsley
1 tsp seasoning salt

Method:

- Preheat oven to 400°F. Prepare a baking sheet by covering it with foil and coating it with non-stick cooking spray.
- Mix flour with the salt and pepper in a small shallow bowl.
- Slice the chicken breasts into pieces that are about 4 inches long and about ½ inch thick. Place them on a large plate.
- Mix the crumbs with the cheese and the seasonings. Place the crumbs in a shallow bowl or on a plate.
- Set up an assembly line consisting of 1. Fresh chicken, 2. Seasoned flour, 3. Melted butter, 4. Parmesan Crumbs and 5. The prepared baking sheet.
- Begin by lightly coating the chicken in the seasoned flour, dipping it in the melted butter, and finish it by completely covering it on both sides with the crumbs. Press it on a little to make sure it is covered.
- Place the coated chicken on the greased baking sheet, making sure they are not too close together, and bake them for about 30 minutes.
- Prepare the Marinara Sauce while the chicken is baking. Recipe on page 64

* To toast the crumbs, spread them out on a baking sheet and bake them at 350 degrees for about 10 to 15 minutes, or until they are golden brown.

Total prep and bake time: about 50 minutes

Note: *After the chicken breasts are breaded they may be kept refrigerated for a day.*

Notes & Quotes

Baked Glazed Ham

Baked Ham is a beautiful thing! There is an air of festivity when you pull a ham out of the oven and place in on a board for presenting and slicing. Even though it isn't hard to do there are some ways to ensure perfection.

- Always purchase high quality ham that is either on the bone or trimmed off the bone. The one pictured is trimmed off the bone.
- Keep the oven low, like at 325° F or lower and be sure not to over bake it.
- Most hams can be baked for 15 minutes per pound.
- Cover the ham and add a little water to the pan so the ham does not dry out.
- Use a simple glaze of apricot jam, stirred up a little, to brush on the ham in the last 20 minutes of the baking time. Uncover the ham for those 20 minutes to get a nice shiny glaze.
- Let the ham rest for a few minutes before slicing it thin and serving it.

Notes & Quotes

"The only time to eat diet food is when you're waiting for the steak to cook."

– Julia Child

Any leftover ham may be chilled, sliced and served cold for awesome sandwiches!

Swedish Meatballs- the Gravy
Makes: 2 cups gravy

Adding a delicious gravy to your meatballs completes the meal. Simply use the frozen meatballs that you so lovingly made and froze for this purpose! This Swedish Meatball recipe has satisfied many appetites at dinners that I have catered.

- Warm about 20 prepared meatballs (recipe page 36) on low heat (300°F) for about 20 minutes.

¼ cup finely diced onions
¼ cup butter
¼ cup flour
1 ½ cups good quality beef broth or homemade*
½ cup half and half, or light cream
1 tsp oregano, crushed

½ tsp paprika
¼ tsp garlic powder
¼ tsp pepper
½ tsp salt or to taste, depending on the beef broth
1 tbsp. fresh chopped parsley

Method:

- Melt the butter in a medium saucepan and sauté the onions in the butter until they are tender.
- Sprinkle the flour over the sizzling butter and onions, stirring gently with a wooden spoon.
- Using a whisk, whisk in the beef broth. Add the broth slowly.
- Cook and stir until the gravy comes to a low boil.
- Add the cream and all the seasonings and mix well just until the gravy comes to a low boil again. If you like the gravy thinner, simply add a little more liquid. This may be broth, water or cream.
- Pour the gravy over the hot meatballs. Serve with Creamy Mashed Potatoes.
- Serve immediately or cover and keep them warm until you are ready to serve them.

Total prep and cooking time: 15 minutes
*using a good quality broth is very important for a delicious result.

Meatballs (Master Recipe)

Makes: 50 meatballs

Meatballs can be made for a meal or used as an appetizer. They are wonderful to have as an option at your party. Guests seem to like having a hot item to pick from at an appetizer table. Meatballs can be made ahead and frozen, making prep time on the day of your party less stressful.

1 ½ lbs. lean ground beef

1 c. fresh bread crumbs, lightly packed, or ½ cup dried bread crumbs

½ tsp Tabasco sauce

1 egg

3 tbsp. ketchup or tomato sauce

1 tbsp. W. Sauce (Worcestershire)

2 tbsp. milk

2 tsp Dijon mustard, optional

2 tbsp. onions chopped fine or grated

1 tbsp. fresh chopped parsley

1 tsp. seasoning salt

¼ tsp. pepper

½ tsp. garlic powder

Method:

- Preheat oven to 400 ° F. Line 2 trays with foil and coat them with non-stick cooking spray.
- Lightly stir the bread crumbs with the ground beef in a large bowl.
- Place the remaining ingredients in a small bowl and stir them together.
- Add the liquid to the ground beef and crumbs. Do not over mix as this will make the meatballs tough.
- Roll into one inch size meatballs. Roll them tight so they stay together.
- Bake the meatballs for about 15 to 20 minutes.
- Place them in your decorative dish and pour over a thick and tangy sweet and sour sauce. (recipe at suchgreatrecipes.com)

Total prep and baking time: about 40 minutes

Notes & Quotes

Note: *Make sure you make extras when you do these; these meatballs will disappear off the baking sheet when you take them out of the oven! I often have to make another tray to make up for the "missing" ones.*

Beef and Bacon Rolls

Makes: 15 rolls

If it has bacon around it, it is going to be good! Bacon gives these rolls a wonderful smoky flavor that compliments the filling. Prepare plenty of these and use them sliced in a sandwich the next day!

1 recipe meatballs (recipe on previous page)   **15 slices uncooked bacon**

Method:

- Form the meat into 1 ½ inch size balls and then form into log shaped rolls.
- Using one slice of bacon per roll, wrap the bacon around the roll.
- Wrap them just to cover the rolls and do not overlap the bacon slice. Trim the bacon off if necessary. (These can be made in the morning and chilled until you are ready to fry them.)
- Starting with a cold skillet, fry the rolls at 350 degrees for a total of 15 to 20 minutes, turning to brown all sides.
- Drizzle with beef gravy if desired.
- Serve with Dill Buttered Baby Carrots (recipe page 61) and Pan Fried Potatoes.

Total prep and cooking time: about 40 minutes

Notes & Quotes

Note: *Bacon rolls can be made into small appetizer size and do not require a sauce.*

Teriyaki Chicken
Makes: 6 servings

After several tries and many willing tasters helping me, I finally came up with a Teriyaki Chicken recipe that has just the right amount of zing and sweetness I was after! Since everyone loves this recipe, the kids make it for their lesson about Hawaii, in my "America Cooks" class. This recipe can be made as a dinner using larger strips or as an appetizer using smaller pieces.

3 chicken breasts (about 6 oz. each)
Marinade and sauce:
6 tbsp. soy sauce
6 tbsp. pineapple juice
3 tbsp. vinegar
3 tbsp. vegetable oil
5 tbsp. packed brown sugar

1 tsp powdered ginger
2 garlic cloves, minced
½ tsp salt
¼ tsp pepper
Thicken with:
2 tsp cornstarch
2 tbsp. water

Method:

- Slice the chicken breasts* into thin strips about ½ inch thick. (For appetizer size, cut the strips again to make one inch pieces) Place the strips or pieces in a bowl.
- Use a glass, liquid measuring cup to mix all the marinade ingredients. Pour *half* of the marinade over the chicken strips and stir it to coat the chicken. Set the other half aside.
- Place the marinated chicken in the fridge, covered, for about 20 minutes, stirring occasionally.
- Heat a large skillet to medium high heat. Add about 1 tablespoon vegetable oil to the skillet.
- Drain the marinated chicken.
- Fry the chicken in a single layer in the heated skillet flipping the pieces over when the edges begin to turn white. Continue cooking the chicken until it is nicely browned.
- While the chicken is browning, combine the cornstarch with the water in a small bowl. Stir it into the reserved marinade to make the sauce.
- Pour the reserved marinade over the browned chicken in the skillet, stirring the chicken and sauce around to thicken the sauce and coat the chicken.
- Serve the Teriyaki Chicken dinner with rice and stir fried vegetables. (Recipe page 61) Or serve it as photographed on page 31, grilled with fresh pineapple and colored peppers.

Total prep and cooking time: 45 minutes including marinating time
*Teriyaki Chicken may be prepared using boneless sliced chicken thighs.

Notes & Quotes

Note: *Place garnish on your platters, candles on your tables, soft music in the background and everything you serve will be three times as special!*

Sausage and Chicken Jambalaya
Makes: 6 servings

Jambalaya! It is kind of fun to say, isn't it? You'll be singing it after you taste it! Everyone gets pretty excited when I start putting this together. It has a fair bit of heat but no one minds at all, there are never leftovers! There's just something adventurous about having **Jambalaya** for dinner. This recipe is all done in the same skillet, but with some browning and removing, sautéing and adding. This **Jambalaya** recipe was something new for my family two years ago, but now it is on the "make often" list! This recipe does double well, just make sure you have a large enough skillet. Join the **Jambalaya** adventure!

1 tbsp. vegetable oil

4 boneless* chicken thighs, seasoned with salt and pepper

1 pound spicy smoked sausage, sliced (Andouille is good)

½ cup diced onions

1 cup red or orange bell pepper, chopped

1 cup green bell pepper, diced

2 cloves of garlic, minced

1- 15 oz. can petite diced tomatoes with the liquid

3 cups chicken broth, low salt variety

1 ½ cups converted rice (I like Uncle Ben's)

1 tsp. paprika

1 tsp. salt

¼ tsp. black pepper

¼ tsp. cayenne pepper, or more to taste

½ cup chopped fresh parsley

Method:

- Heat the oil in a large skillet on medium high heat. (An 11" size works well.)
- Have all the vegetables and sausage chopped and ready to go into the skillet.
- Brown the chicken thighs on both sides. Remove them from the skillet and set them aside. Drain off most of the grease from the skillet.
- Place the sausage in the skillet and fry it until it is golden. Remove the sausage and set it aside as well.
- Add the onions, peppers and garlic to the skillet and sauté them for about 3 minutes.
- Stir in the tomatoes, rice, sausage, chicken broth and all the seasonings except the fresh parsley.
- When the mixture comes to a boil place the chicken thighs in the skillet. Cover and simmer until the liquids are almost absorbed, about 30 minutes.
- Remove the chicken from the skillet. Chop the chicken carefully, and since it is very hot, it works best to use a fork to hold the chicken. Add the chopped chicken to the skillet.
- Stir in the fresh parsley and it is ready to serve!

Total prep and cook time: 1 hour

*Bone-in chicken thighs work as well, just remove the bones when you cut up the chicken.

Note: *If you double this recipe and happen to have leftovers, Jambalaya is very good warmed up!*

Notes & Quotes

Grilled Chicken Caesar

Serves: 6

Grilled Chicken Caesar Breasts combine well with a side of rice pilaf and
some sautéed peppers, or corn on the cob and potato salad. Slice them up
and place them on your Caesar Salad for a light lunch option.

6 small chicken breasts, about 5 oz. each
½ cup vegetable oil
2 tbsp. rice vinegar (plain is OK too)
3 tbsp. fresh squeezed lemon juice, (plus
  optional 1 to 2 tbsp. extra for topping)
2 tsp garlic powder
¼ tsp pepper

1 ½ tsp salt
¾ tsp crushed basil
¾ tsp crushed oregano
2 tsp dried parsley flakes
Drizzle and Topping:
½ cup prepared Caesar salad dressing
¼ cup fresh Parmesan curls

Method:

- Place all the marinade ingredients in a heavy duty gallon size zip lock bag.
- Zip up the bag securely and swish the ingredients together to combine them.
- While holding the bag upright, drop the chicken breasts into the marinade. Seal the bag again.
- Shake the chicken breasts with the marinade. Place the bag flat in the refrigerator. Flip it once in a while to distribute the flavors.
- The chicken may be marinated for one to three hours. If you are short on time, let the chicken breasts rest in the marinade for 20 minutes at room temperature. (do not forget to set the timer, any longer and the chicken may not be safe to use)
- Prepare the grill by brushing the grates with oil a few minutes before the chicken goes on. Preheat the grill and drain the chicken breasts so they are not dripping.
- Grill the chicken breasts at about 350 degrees for 5 minutes on each side. You may choose to squeeze some additional fresh lemon juice on the breasts just before they are done. This gives them a nice "tang".
- Place the **Grilled Chicken Caesar** on a serving plate and drizzle the prepared dressing over all the pieces.
- Top with the fresh Parmesan Curls and serve immediately.

Total prep and cooking time: about 30 minutes

Note: *These chicken breasts may be fried in a frying pan on medium heat for about 5 minutes on each side*

Notes & Quotes

Evelyn's Gyros
Makes: 6 Gyros

Anything that is loaded with tangy sauce that oozes out with every bite is going to be my favorite! After trying Gyros from a food truck, I decided to come up with my own version. The results proved positive for my household.

6 plain Pitas, warmed
2 pounds thinly sliced, marinated and cooked beef
3 cups finely shredded cabbage, with oil to soften it slightly
2 cups shredded lettuce
3 cups Tzatziki sauce (recipe page 15)
1 ½ cups crumbled feta cheese
Additional fresh squeezed lemon juice
Salt and pepper

Garlic powder
Oregano
Greek Beef Strips Marinade:
2 tbsp. lemon juice
¼ cup red wine vinegar
¼ cup olive oil
2 cloves minced garlic
2 tsp oregano
½ tsp black pepper
1 tsp salt

Method:

- Whisk together all the marinade and place it in a large zip lock bag with the thinly sliced beef.
- Marinate the beef for at least an hour or overnight.
- Prepare a large skillet for the beef by heating to as hot as it goes and adding 1 tbsp. of oil. Make sure the skillet is large enough to brown all the strips.
- Drain off all the marinade from the beef.
- Place the beef strips into the hot skillet being sure to spread out the strips so they are not double.
- Brown the beef on both sides. While the beef is browning, season it with a little salt, pepper, garlic powder and oregano.
- When the beef is very brown on both sides, drizzle it with some extra lemon juice. (About 3 tbsp.) The beef benefits from the browning and becomes quite tender so don't be afraid of over browning it!
- After the beef has sizzled with the added lemon juice, remove it from the pan to serve it.
- Layer the toppings on the warmed pitas.

Total prep and cooking time: 45 minutes to 1 hour

Note: *This may be served without the pita bread to make a Greek Beef and Cabbage Dinner.*

Spaghetti Sauce-Cooking Class Favorite

Serves 6

This Spaghetti Sauce received raves from my students; and that at 10 o' clock in the morning!

1 tbsp. vegetable oil
¼ cup finely chopped onions
1 large garlic clove, minced
1 pound lean ground beef
1- 24 oz. jar spaghetti sauce*

1 tsp Italian seasoning
1 tsp dried parsley flakes
1- 1 pound package spaghetti noodles (thin is best)
Parmesan cheese

Method:

- Begin by boiling the water for the noodles. Add the noodles when the water is boiling.
- Sauté the onions and the garlic with the ground beef. Cook and break apart the ground beef until it is all browned. Drain off any accumulated fat.
- Stir in the spaghetti sauce and the seasoning and cook until the sauce comes to a low boil.
- Drain the cooked noodles and pour the sauce over the pasta.
- Serve hot with a sprinkling of Parmesan cheese and Garlic Toast

*Using a good quality pasta and sauce is always important.

Total prep and cook time: 30 minutes

Chicken Curry

Serves: 6

Slow baked Chicken Curry has so much flavor and tenderness, it practically melts in your mouth! I am always excited to make and eat this dish! I like to make plenty so I can have it for lunch for a few days afterwards. Never mind the curry aroma that hangs on for a few days!

8 chicken thigh sections, trimmed of excess fat
Coat chicken in:
¼ cup flour
1 tsp salt
¼ tsp pepper
Top browned chicken with:
1 ½ cups chopped pepper (any colors)
½ cup chopped onions
2 small garlic cloves, minced

2 small carrots, chopped
3 stalks celery, chopped
1 unpeeled, cored and diced apple
Mix together:
2 to 3 tbsp. curry powder
1 ½ cups chicken broth
1 tsp salt
⅛ tsp pepper

Method:

- Preheat your oven to 325°F.
- Coat the trimmed chicken pieces in the flour mixture. Tossing all the thighs into a large zip lock bag with the flour is a quick way to evenly coat the chicken.
- Brown the coated chicken on both sides in a skillet with a little butter or vegetable oil. This takes about 15 minutes.
- Place the browned chicken thighs in a Dutch oven pan or roasting dish.
- Cover the chicken with the chopped vegetables and apples.
- Combine the curry with the salt, pepper and broth and pour it over the chicken and vegetables.
- Jiggle the pan a little to make sure the chicken pieces settle into the juices.
- Bake the Chicken Curry covered for one and a half hours at 325°F.
- Serve the juicy chicken with hot cooked rice. The juices are not too thick so they pour nicely over the rice.

Total prep and baking time: 2 hours

Note: *This dinner may be completely baked and chilled for up to 3 days. Reheat it in a low oven (300° F) for 45 minutes to an hour.*

Linguine Alfredo

Yield: 6 to 8 servings

Since we all love plenty of sauce on our pasta, I created an Alfredo sauce that is just a little lighter. Water is added to it to cut down on the heavy cream content, but the addition of white wine gives it plenty of flavor. Linguine is the pasta of choice here because it is lighter as well.

1 pound Linguine
¼ cup butter
1 garlic clove, minced
2 tbsp. minced onion
3 tbsp. flour
1 cup water

1 cup heavy cream
2 tbsp. dry white wine
¼ tsp pepper
½ tsp salt
1 tbsp. dried parsley flakes
1 cup fresh grated Parmesan cheese, divided

Method:

- Cook the linguine in boiling water for 8 minutes or until it is done.
- Cook the onions and garlic in the butter for about 3 minutes or until the onions are slightly tender.
- Sprinkle the flour over the cooking onions and garlic and stir it well.
- Whisk it carefully while you add the water and cream to ensure there are no lumps.
- When the mixture comes to a boil, add the wine, the seasonings and ¾ cup of the Parmesan cheese. Remove it from the heat. The sauce will thicken more as it stands.
- Drain the linguine when it is cooked and let it rest until the sauce is ready.
- Pour the completed sauce over the cooked noodles and garnish it with the additional ¼ cup Parmesan and some fresh ground pepper.
- Cooked chicken or smoked salmon may be added to the sauce or placed on each serving.

Total prep and cook time: 30 minutes

Notes & Quotes

Note: *Give the sauce a basil garlic twist with an addition of Spinach and Basil Pesto recipe page 64.*

Skillet Salmon

Serves: 6

By adding sautéed mushrooms, a delightful spinach in cream sauce and Lemon and Dill Rice, you have a mouthwatering dish! Pan frying the salmon takes less than ten minutes and the rest can easily be put together in short order as well. The presentation is impressive, so it makes an awesome dinner to serve a small dinner party, but Skillet Salmon may be served with any side dishes you desire.

6 - 5 oz. pieces of filleted salmon, skin removed
1 to 2 tsp Old Bay seasoning
½ tsp dill

4 tsp butter
<u>Garnish and Topping:</u>
Lemon wedges and a squeeze of lemon

Method:

- Season the salmon with the Old Bay Seasoning and the dill on both sides.
- Heat the skillet to medium high heat to melt the 4 tsp butter until it is sizzling.
- Place the salmon, best side down, into the hot skillet.
- Set the timer for 4 minutes and flip the fillets over and set the timer for another 4 minutes.
- Turn the heat off under the salmon when it is done.
- Squeeze some fresh lemon over the salmon and place a small lemon wedge beside the fillet or on the rice.

Total prep and cook time: 10 minutes
Recipe for rice page 59, recipe for spinach page 62.

Oven Baked BBQ Pork Spare Ribs

Makes: 6 to 8 servings

The great thing about oven baking for a BBQ flavor is that you can do this year round. These ribs are in the oven very low for four hours. This makes them nice and tender with just a little "chew". Prepare plenty of them and serve them with your favorite rolls, potato salad and perhaps corn on the cob.

3 to 4 pounds boneless pork spare ribs

Rub:

½ cup brown sugar

2 tbsp. white sugar

1 tsp garlic powder

1 tsp paprika

1 tsp chili powder

¼ tsp pepper

1 tsp salt

Sauce:

1 cup BBQ sauce (Sweet Baby Ray's is my favorite)

¼ cup ketchup

¼ cup white sugar

1 tbsp. vinegar

Pinch of cayenne or more to taste

Method:

- Preheat the oven to 250° F. Spray a baking sheet with non-stick cooking spray.
- Combine all the rub ingredients in a small bowl.
- Spread the rub on a large plate and roll the ribs in it to cover them.
- Place the covered ribs on the greased baking sheet in the preheated oven.
- Bake the ribs, uncovered for 2 hours.
- Meanwhile, prepare the sauce by stirring all the ingredients in a small bowl. Set the bowl aside
- Spread the BBQ sauce on the ribs and "tent" a piece of foil over them and bake them for another 2 hours.

Total prep and bake time: 4 hours; plan ahead!

Note: *Make some extra sauce to change this into a sandwich filling! Simply shred the pork and stir in the sauce.*

Notes & Quotes

Pollo a la Crema

Serves: 6

A la Mexicana! Pollo a la Crema has moist chicken pieces in a creamy, distinctive Mexican flavored sauce. This recipe was created after dining at several Mexican restaurants. I like to combine all my favorites and come up with a version that will be enjoyed by everyone. The clean plates testify of a mission accomplished! Aside from the time the chicken needs to marinade, this dish can be completed in less than a half hour.

2 large chicken breasts, sliced into thin strips
Marinade:
2 tbsp. vegetable oil
1 tbsp. rice vinegar, or regular vinegar
½ tsp garlic powder
⅛ tsp pepper
½ tsp seasoning salt
Add:
1 tbsp. butter
½ cup onion slices

1 large clove of garlic, minced
Sauce:
1 cup heavy cream
1 ½ tbsp. chicken broth concentrate or granules
5 tbsp. tomato paste
2 tsp hot sauce or more to suit your taste
1 tsp dried cilantro
Salt and pepper to taste
1 tbsp. cold butter

Method:

- Marinate the sliced chicken for about 20 minutes.
- Heat an electric skillet and add the 1 tbsp. butter.
- Drain the chicken strips and place them in the heated skillet to brown them. This takes about 5 minutes. Be careful not to overcook the chicken.
- Flip the chicken strips so that the browned side is up. Add the sliced onions and the garlic.
- Cook the chicken with the garlic and onions for about 3 minutes.
- Pour the heavy cream over the chicken and stir it around to heat it to a simmer. This only takes a couple minutes.
- In a small bowl, whisk the chicken broth concentrate with the tomato paste, hot sauce and the seasoning.
- Stir the tomato sauce mixture into the simmering cream and chicken.
- Cook the chicken in the sauce until it comes to a low boil.
- Stir in the 1 tbsp. cold butter and continue cooking it until the sauce is slightly thickened.
- Keep the Pollo a la Crema on low heat until you are ready to serve it.

Total prep and cook time: 40 minutes

Notes & Quotes

Note: *All the "fixings" for this dinner may be placed in a warm tortilla as well.*

Mexican Theme Dinner Menu

Tortilla chips with salsa and Guacamole (page 59)
Fresh Strawberry Margaritas (page 108)
Pollo a la Crema
Spanish rice (page 59)
Sautéed Colored Peppers
Cinnamon Tortilla Crisps (suchgreatrecipes.com)

Mock Chicken Cordon Bleu
Makes: 4 or 5 servings

Chicken Cordon Bleu always sounds gourmet and difficult. It can stay gourmet, but it does not need to be difficult. This sneaky way of simply layering the cheese and ham between breaded chicken breast slices gives you the same tasty results and impressive presentation that everyone loves.

Chicken:
2 large chicken breasts sliced very thin
Flour coating:
½ tsp salt
¼ pepper
½ cup flour
Dip into:
½ cup melted butter, or more as needed

Crumb Coating:
3 cups dry bread crumbs
1 tsp garlic powder
1 tbsp. dried parsley
½ tsp black pepper
1 tsp salt
10 slices Black Forest Ham
20 slices Swiss cheese
Butter and oil for the skillet

Method:

- To achieve ½ inch thick slices, run your knife across the bottom of the chicken breast while pressing on it firmly with your other hand. Keep your knife level to keep the slice even.
- Make each slice the same size by trimming them to the size you'd like them to be. You should end up with 8 to 10 slices.
- Dip the slices in the flour, then the melted butter and finally into the crumb mixture. Make sure both sides are well coated.
- Prepare the electric skillet by heating it to 375° F. Place 2 tbsp. butter and 1 tbsp. oil in the skillet. Preheat the oven to 350 degrees and spray a baking sheet with non-stick cooking spray.
- When the butter and oil are hot and melted, not browned, place the breaded slices in the skillet to cook them.
- Flip the chicken slices when the edges are getting white, about 4 minutes on each side.
- Place half of the browned chicken breasts on the prepared baking sheet.
- Layer the cheese and the ham over the chicken on the baking sheet, starting and ending with cheese.
- Top each of them with a fitting chicken piece.
- Place the completed Chicken Cordon Bleu in the oven and bake them for about 10 minutes or until the cheese is melted.
- While the chicken is heating, prepare cheese sauce to pour over the completed chicken. (recipe page 63)

Total prep, cooking and baking time: about 1 hour including making the sauce.

Make it French Tonight!
Menu

French Cream of Tomato Soup (page 24)
Sparkling White Grape Punch (page 112) or white wine
Chicken Cordon Bleu
Wild Rice Pilaf (page 58)
Garden Vegetables
Mocha Filled Lace Cookies (page 96)

Cabbage Rice Dinner with Jalapenos
Makes: 6 servings

Healthy and quick to put together, this dinner is amazingly well received!
Even when you enjoy cooking, there are days when there are just too many other things to do! **Cabbage Rice Dinner** has everything you need to make a complete dinner in one dish.

3 cups cabbage, cut in short strips
½ cup chopped red pepper
½ cup chopped yellow pepper
1 cup carrots, cut into small slivers
¼ cup chopped onions
1 clove garlic, minced
1 whole jalapeno, seeded and chopped fine
½ pound cooked ground beef, crumbled

1 cup converted rice
1 tsp salt
¼ tsp pepper
2 ¼ cups hot, lower sodium chicken broth
Topping:
1 ½ cup shredded cheddar cheese
¾ cup sour cream

Method:

- Preheat oven to 350 degrees. Prepare an 8 x 10 by 2 ½ inch baking dish by spraying it with non-stick cooking spray.
- Place all the chopped vegetables, ground beef, rice and salt and pepper in a large bowl. Toss it together lightly.
- Place the vegetable combination in the prepared baking dish and press it in firmly.
- Pour the hot chicken broth over the vegetables and beef.
- Cover and bake for 1 hour.
- Stir the sour cream with the shredded cheddar in a small bowl.
- Remove the dinner from the oven and drop spoons full of the cheddar cheese topping on it. Return the baked dinner to the oven and bake, covered, for 10 more minutes.
- Total cook and prep time: about 1 ½ hours

The Accompaniments–Potatoes, Rice, Vegetables and Sauces

Having been raised on many fresh vegetables from my Papa's abundant garden, I learned the importance of eating plenty of them! The vegetables, potatoes, rice and sauces included in this chapter are all essentials to a complete meal.

Oven Baked Wild Rice Pilaf

Makes: 15 to 20 servings

Rice Pilaf that has been baked in the oven is quite similar to the stove top kind. Baking it in the oven gives it a wonderful texture and it is almost never sticky. The addition of an abundance of vegetables makes it colorful and flavorful. Wild Rice Pilaf has been on many buffet tables and there are always positive comments about it! Be sure to measure all the ingredients to ensure fully cooked rice.

1 medium carrot, chopped fine
1 stick of celery, chopped fine
⅓ cup chopped onions
½ cup chopped colored peppers
2 tbsp. butter
1 tsp vegetable oil
2 ½ cups converted rice (Uncle Ben's is good)

⅓ cup wild rice (presoaked)*
2 tbsp. parsley flakes, crumbled
¼ tsp thyme, crumbled
½ tsp salt or more, depending on sodium in chicken broth
¼ tsp pepper
6 cups boiled chicken broth

Method:

- Preheat oven to 350º F. Prepare a 10 to 12 cup capacity casserole dish by spraying it well with non-stick cooking spray.
- Start by bringing the chicken broth to a boil.
- While the broth is coming to a boil, chop all the vegetables and sauté them briefly in the butter and oil. They only need to be sautéed for about 5 minutes.
- Add the rice and the seasoning to the sautéed vegetables. Stir to make the mixture thoroughly combined and nice and shiny!
- Scrape out the rice and vegetables into the prepared casserole dish.
- Pour the hot chicken stock over the rice very carefully. Stir very gently with a wooden spoon.
- Cover the dish with 2 layers of foil that have been greased to prevent rice from sticking to it. Make sure the edges are sealed well.
- Bake the Wild Rice Pilaf for 45 minutes to an hour. Check the rice at the 45 minute mark to see if it has gained volume and all the liquid is absorbed. Remove it from the oven if it is cooked.
- Carefully remove the foil and lightly toss the Wild Rice Pilaf with a fork to stir together all those wonderful colors and to release some wonderful aromas!

*presoak the wild rice for at least 2 hours before using it. Simply cover it with water and then strain it before using.
Total prep and baking time: 1 ½ hours Photo on page 55 with Cordon Bleu.

Note: *This is quite a large recipe so you will probably have leftovers. Rice is easy to reheat and sautéing it is the best way. Use a skillet with some melted butter and stir the rice around gently until it is heated through.*

Notes & Quotes

Spanish Rice
Makes: 4 cups rice

The perfect accompaniment to your Mexican inspired dishes.

½ cup ground tomatoes
2 ½ cups chicken broth

1 tsp hot sauce
1 ½ cups converted rice (I prefer Uncle Ben's)

Method:

- Bring the chicken broth, hot sauce and ground tomatoes to a boil in a medium size saucepan.
- Add the rice and return to a boil.
- After rice comes to a boil, turn the heat to low.
- Cover and simmer the rice for 25 minutes or until all the liquid is absorbed.
- Toss lightly with a fork and serve with your favorite Mexican dish.

Total prep and cook time: 30 minutes Photo on page 53 with Pollo a la Crema

---

Lemon and Dill Rice

Makes: 4 cups rice

3 cups chicken broth
1 tbsp. butter
1 ½ cups long grain converted rice
2 tbsp. lemon juice

1 tsp dill
⅛ tsp pepper
1 tbsp. butter (after cooking)

Method:

- Bring the chickens stock and the first tablespoon of butter to a boil.
- Add the rice and cook until the rice comes to a boil again.
- Cover the rice and turn it to very low heat and let it simmer for 25 minutes.
- After the rice is cooked, add the additional 1 tbsp. butter, the lemon juice, the pepper and the dill. Use a fork to stir it carefully. Serve it hot.

Total prep and cook time: 40 minutes
Photo page 49 with the Skillet Salmon

Notes & Quotes

Note: *We have a little note on how to remember not to peek at rice while it is cooking. I told my daughter that rice needs to stay covered while it is cooking. She says, "Oh, I get it, rice likes its privacy!" So we call it private rice to remember this.*

Creamy Mashed Potatoes to Make Ahead

Makes: 12 servings

Any dish that can be made ahead helps you relax a little and enjoy your festivities with your family and friends. Whether you make these creamy potatoes using the reds or using peeled Russets, they are sure to please all. Even when I make a large batch of these it seems they are always all eaten! The guests come back for second *and* third helpings!

5 pounds red potatoes, skins on
½ tsp salt
¾ cups butter
1 – 8 oz. package cream cheese, softened

½ cup half and half
1 tsp seasoning salt
½ tsp pepper
½ tsp garlic powder (optional)

Method:

- Cut the potatoes into even size chunks. Wash them and place them in a large cooking pot.
- Cook the potatoes in water, barely covering them, and add ½ tsp of the salt to the pot.
- After the potatoes come to a boil, cover them and keep them boiling on low heat for about 30 minutes or until they are tender when tested with a fork.
- Drain the potatoes well, and place them back on the low heat to dry them further.
- Mash the potatoes while they are still on low heat to allow all the steam to escape before adding the other ingredients.
- Remove the potatoes from the heat and add all the remaining ingredients.
- Mash them very well until they are smooth and creamy. They may be served at this point if you rather not bake them.
- Place them in a large greased baking dish. Place a few pats of butter on top and either bake them immediately or cover and chill them to bake later.
- To bake them immediately, place them in a 350° oven for about 20 minutes or until the butter is melted and the potatoes are heated through.
- When making this dish a day or two in advance, take them out of the fridge about an hour before baking them. Bake them at 350° covered with a lid or parchment and then aluminum foil. Bake them for 30 to 40 minutes or until heated through. You will know they are ready when they are easy to stir around in the middle of the baking dish.

Total prep and baking time: about 1 ½ hours or 40 minutes if you choose not to bake them. Photo on the chapter title page.

Dill Buttered Baby Carrots

1 pound baby carrots, smallest you can find
½ tsp salt

2 tbsp. butter
1 tsp dill

Method:

- Cook the baby carrots in about an inch of water and the salt.
- When the water boils, turn the heat low and cook for 15 minutes more or until the carrots are crisp-tender.
- Drain the carrots and keep them on low while you add the butter and dill.
- Toss the carrots in the pan gently and remove them from the heat.
- Serve them immediately.

Quick Vegetable Stir Fry
Makes: 6 servings

Prepare these vegetables while your Teriyaki Chicken is cooking to perfection.

3 carrots
1 onion
1 orange bell pepper

½ head of cabbage
Salt and pepper to taste

Method:

- Slice all the vegetables into equal sized strips.
- Place them in a lightly oiled and heated skillet or Wok.
- Cook them until they wilt slightly but are still crisp, tossing them to ensure even cooking, about 10 minutes. Season with the salt and pepper.
- Serve them with the Teriyaki Chicken.

Total prep and cook time: about 20 minutes Photo page 39

"A good cook works by the fire of imagination, not merely by the fire in the stove".
– Robert P. Tristram, Coffin

Spinach with Garlic Cream Sauce

Makes: 6 servings

A Garlic Cream Sauce is delightful with spinach, it is so wonderfully creamy and full of flavor!

10 oz. bag of baby spinach
1 ½ tbsp. butter
1 tbsp. minced onions
1 garlic clove, minced

1 tbsp. flour
½ cup chicken broth
½ cup cream (half and half)
Salt and fresh pepper to taste

Method:

- Cook 10 ounces of baby spinach in a large pot just until the spinach wilts.
- Drain the spinach well, set it aside and prepare the sauce.
- For the sauce: Melt the butter in a small saucepan until it is bubbly.
- Add the onions and garlic and sauté them for about 3 minutes.
- Sprinkle the flour over the cooking butter and onions and stir it well.
- Slowly pour in the broth and the cream, while stirring, to make a thick creamy sauce.
- Season with the salt and pepper and stir the sauce into the cooked and drained spinach. Pictured under the Skillet Salmon on page 49.

Total prep time: 10 minutes

Notes & Quotes

My Papa enjoying his lush garden that kept us all nourished for so many years!

Creamy Cheese Sauce

Makes: 2 cups sauce

Having a good sauce can really enhance the flavor and appearance of a dish. And, having a good sauce can really *hide* the flavor and appearance of a dish! Cheese sauce is good on a variety of vegetables but is perfect on the **Chicken Cordon Bleu**. I like to use broth and cream instead of milk in this sauce because it gives a creamier texture and it does not have the sweetness that milk brings.

2 tbsp. butter
2 tbsp. flour
¼ to ½ tsp salt
⅛ tsp pepper

1 cup chicken broth or water
½ cup half and half
1 ½ cup shredded cheddar cheese or Swiss

Method:

- In a medium saucepan, melt the butter.
- When the butter bubbles a little, sprinkle the flour over it.
- Cook the flour and butter for about a minute.
- Add the salt and pepper, and then slowly add the liquids while stirring constantly.
- When the sauce comes to a light boil, stir in the shredded cheese.
- Turn the heat to low and stir the sauce until the cheese is melted.
- Add salt or any desired seasonings as needed. Serve immediately.

Total prep time: about 10 minutes. Photograph on page 55 over the Cordon Bleu

"People who love to eat are always the best people".

– Julia Child

Notes & Quotes

Italian Marinara Sauce

Makes: 3 cups sauce

An awesome dip for breadsticks or for topping the Oven Baked Parmesan Chicken.

1 tbsp. olive oil
¼ cup finely chopped onions
1 garlic clove, minced
2 cups tomato sauce (15 oz. can)
1- 6 oz. can tomato paste
1 tsp oregano, crushed

1 tsp basil, crushed
¼ tsp pepper
salt to taste
1 tbsp. parmesan cheese plus 2 tbsp. fresh for
 topping

Method:

- In a small saucepan sauté the onions with the garlic in the olive oil.
- When the onions are tender add the sauces and seasonings. Cook and stir until the sauce begins to bubble.
- Remove the sauce from the heat and add the Parmesan cheese.
- Pour the sauce over the baked Parmesan chicken breasts and garnish with fresh grated parmesan and some chopped parsley. Or use as a dipping sauce for the Parmesan and Herb Breadsticks.

Total prep and cooking time: about 15 minutes. Photo page 33

Spinach and Basil Pesto

Makes: ⅔ cup pesto

Add a few scoops of Pesto to your Alfredo Sauce and use this in the Italian Salami Pinwheels.

1 clove garlic
½ cup cooked spinach
¼ cup parmesan cheese,
2 tbsp. vegetable oil

¼ tsp pepper
¼ tsp salt
2 tbsp. dried basil

Method:

- In a small food processor or a blender process all ingredients until the pesto is very smooth. Total prep time: 5 minutes.

Muffins and Quick Breads

I was told that, the smell of fresh baked muffins helps my daughter get out of bed in the morning. That along with coffee aromas wafting in, will give a definite pull! We have tested these muffin recipes over and over and made several deliveries of them when a bit of comforting was needed.

"Doughnut" Mini Muffins
Makes: 24 mini muffins

Have you ever waited in line for those mini doughnuts that you find at special events? These mini muffins resemble them. They are the perfect two bites of cinnamon and sugary goodness! Morning coffee with a few Doughnut Mini Muffins is such a sweet way to begin your day!

⅓ cup butter	1 ½ tsp baking powder
½ cup sugar	½ tsp salt
1 tsp vanilla	¼ tsp nutmeg
1 egg	½ tsp cinnamon
1 ½ cups flour	½ cup milk

Method:

- Preheat oven to 350 degrees F. Spray a mini muffin tin (to make 24), with non-stick cooking spray.
- In a large bowl, using an electric mixer, beat the butter with the sugar until it is light and fluffy.
- Add the vanilla and the egg and continue beating. Set the bowl aside to prepare the flour mixture.
- Whisk together the dry ingredients in a medium bowl.
- Always start and end with flour when adding to your creamed butter.
- Start by adding one third of the flour mixture to the beaten butter and egg. Beat just until combined.
- Add half of the milk, beat, and then another third of the flour.
- Add the rest of the milk and end with the last third of flour. Do not over mix.
- Drop the batter into the greased muffin tins, filling them about ⅔ full.
- Bake them for 13 minutes. If you make 24 mini muffins, they take exactly 13 minutes to be done!
- Melt the butter and make the sugar mixture while you are waiting for the "doughnuts" to bake.

In a small bowl melt:

½ cup butter

Mix together in another small bowl:

¾ cup sugar
1 ½ tsp cinnamon

- When the muffins are fresh out of the oven, coat them in butter and immediately roll them in the sugar.
- Work quickly so you can serve them when they are still warm.

Total prep and bake time: about 45 minutes

Note: These **Doughnut Mini Muffins** *taste just as good the next day warmed up ever so slightly.*

Notes & Quotes

Apple and Carrot Muffins
Makes: 12 muffins

Muffins are meant to be somewhat healthy. Apples, carrots, nuts and some whole wheat flour, that's pretty healthy I think! Cream cheese frosting? Sure! These muffins are moist enough without the cream cheese frosting, but the tangy topping *is* a wonderful addition!

Dry ingredients:
¾ cup flour
¼ cup whole wheat flour
½ tsp baking soda
½ tsp baking powder
¼ tsp salt
½ tsp cinnamon

Liquid ingredients:
¾ cup brown sugar
½ cup vegetable oil
2 eggs
1 ½ cups shredded* apple (about 2 apples)
1 ½ cups finely shredded carrots (about 1 ½ carrots)
¼ cup chopped nuts

Method:

- Preheat oven to 350°F. Spray a regular size muffin tin with non-stick cooking spray.
- Begin by placing all the dry ingredients in a small bowl. (First 6 ingredients) Whisk together carefully.
- In a large bowl place the sugar, vegetable oil, eggs, shredded apples, the carrots and the nuts. Stir this together well, using a wooden spoon or a spatula.
- Pour the dry ingredients into the large bowl with the apple and carrot mixture. Stir well to completely moisten the batter. Be careful to not over mix as this will result in a tougher textured muffin.
- Scoop the batter into the muffin tin to make 12 muffins.
- Bake for 20 minutes. Let the muffins rest for about 10 minutes in the tins before removing them to a cooling rack. Prepare cream cheese frosting. Recipe at suchgreatrecipes.com
- Pipe or spread the frosting onto warm muffins to serve immediately. They can also be frosted when they are chilled and stored in a sealed container for a few days.

Total prep and baking time: 45 minutes
*I have found that shredding apples rather than chopping them gives these muffins a more even texture. You get all the moisture and flavor without any "pockets" of air.

Honey Bran Muffins
Makes: 12 muffins

Several years ago (ok, lots of years), in a Foods class, I was required to compile recipes to make a recipe box collection. This recipe came out of there and it is quite amazing that I got this recipe to turn out, since the sketched instructions were quite vague! But, they turn out every time and we love having them for breakfast or as an afternoon snack.

¼ cup butter

½ cup packed dark brown sugar

¼ cup molasses

2 eggs

1 cup milk

1 tsp vanilla

Dry Ingredients:

1 cup flour

1 ½ cups wheat bran

1 ½ tsp baking powder

½ tsp baking soda

¾ tsp salt

(½ cup diced apples, raisins or chocolate chips)

2 tbsp. honey to drizzle on top

Method:

- Preheat oven to 400°F. Prepare a muffin tin by lining them with paper cups. Lightly spray the whole pan with non-stick cooking spray to make the papers easy to remove.
- Beat the butter with the brown sugar. Add the molasses and beat until it is smooth.
- Add the eggs one at a time, beating well after each addition.
- Pour in the milk and vanilla and beat it until combined. (The consistency of the liquid will be curdled)
- Stir together the dry ingredients in a separate bowl.
- Add the dry ingredients to the liquid ingredients using a wooden spoon to combine them well without over mixing.
- If you desire to add apples, raisins or chocolate chips, stir them in now.
- Scoop the batter into the prepared tins, filling 12 cups about ¾ full.
- Bake them for about 16 to 18 minutes.
- Use a "honey bear" to drizzle some honey over each muffin.
- Serve them warm with plenty of butter.

Total prep and baking time: 40 minutes

Citrus Zucchini Muffins

Makes: 12 muffins

Another delicious way to put away another zucchini or two, because no-one
seems to have enough recipes to use up their endless zucchini supply!

¼ cup vegetable oil

¼ cup melted butter

¾ cup packed brown sugar

1 tbsp. honey

2 small eggs

1 tsp vanilla

2 tsp orange zest

2 tsp lemon zest

2 tsp cinnamon

⅓ cup grated apples

1 cup grated zucchini

3 tbsp. buttermilk

<u>Dry Ingredients:</u>

1 ⅔ cups flour

2 tsp baking powder

¼ tsp baking soda

½ tsp salt

Method:

- Line a muffin tin with paper liners. Preheat the oven to 375° F.
- In a medium size bowl, mix all the liquid ingredients, up to and including the buttermilk. Stir them together with a fork.
- In another bowl, whisk together all the dry ingredients.
- Add the liquids to the dry and use a fork to incorporate them well. Be careful not to over mix the batter.
- Scoop the muffin batter into the prepared tin and bake the muffins for about 20 minutes.
- After removing the muffins from the tins let them rest for 10 minutes before glazing them.

Glaze:

1 cup powdered sugar

1 tsp fresh squeezed lemon juice

1 to 2 tbsp. fresh squeezed orange
  juice

- Stir together the glaze in a small bowl adding the orange juice slowly until you have a glaze thick enough to adhere to the top of the muffin.
- The muffins may be dipped twice to get a thicker glaze.

Total prep and baking time: 40 minutes

Streusel Topped Blueberry Oat Muffins

Makes: 12 muffins

If we could post a scent with a photo, this one would be a winner! Streusel Topped Blueberry Oat Muffins make an awesome breakfast, but are equally good for a midnight snack while doing homework. (Thus commented my overwhelmed with homework daughter!)

1 ⅓ cups flour
½ cup oat bran
2 tsp baking powder
½ tsp baking soda
½ tsp salt
¾ cup milk
½ cup packed brown sugar
1 egg, lightly beaten

⅓ cup melted butter
½ tsp vanilla extract
1 to 1 ½ cups fresh or frozen blueberries
Streusel:
2 tbsp. flour
2 tbsp. packed brown sugar
1 tsp oat bran
2 tbsp. cold butter

Method:

- Preheat the oven to 400° F. Prepare a muffin tin by lining it with cupcake liners.
- Combine the dry ingredients in a medium size bowl.
- Whisk together the milk, egg, brown sugar, melted butter and the vanilla in a small bowl.
- Use a fork to stir the liquid into the dry ingredients. Add the blueberries to the batter as you lightly moisten the dry ingredients.
- Be very careful when combining the liquid with the dry ingredients. The batter will not seem to be mixed but it all works out!
- Scoop the batter into the prepared muffin tin to make 10 large muffins or 12 medium sized.
- Prepare the streusel in a small bowl using a knife to cut it into crumbs.
- Sprinkle the streusel on top of the muffins using your fingers to crumble it.
- Bake the muffins for 18 to 20 minutes depending on how many you made. Enjoy the wonderful scent of these baking!
- Serve them warm with butter or let them come to room temperature and freeze them for another day!

Total prep and baking time: 45 minutes

Notes & Quotes

Note: *Double your muffin tins so the bottom of the muffins do not get too dark.*

Biscuit "Croissants" with Vanilla Cream

Makes: 1 dozen

These "croissants" look like you spent hours making them, but are really quite quick and easy. The creamy filling is a delicious surprise.

Filling:
3 oz. cream cheese
2 tbsp. sugar
1 tsp clear vanilla
Dry ingredients:
1 ¾ cups flour
1 tsp salt
1 tbsp. baking powder

2 tbsp. sugar
Add:
⅓ cup cold unsalted butter, cut up
Then add:
⅔ cup milk
Egg Wash:
1 egg yolk
1 tbsp. milk

Method:

- Preheat oven to 375°F. Prepare a baking sheet by lightly spraying it with non-stick cooking spray.
- For the filling: beat the cream cheese with the sugar and vanilla until it is smooth. Set the bowl aside.
- Stir together the dry ingredients in a large bowl, or use a food processor.
- Cut in or use a food processor to blend in the butter and mix it until it resembles fine crumbs. Place the crumbs in a large bowl.
- Make a well in the center and pour in the milk. Stir gently with a fork just to moisten. Knead the dough about 8 times or until it is smooth.
- Use your hands to form the dough into two balls. On a lightly floured surface, roll the dough into two 9 inch circles.
- Cut each circle into six wedges. Place a portion of the vanilla cream on the wide half of each wedge.
- Roll the wedge croissant style; wide edge to narrow edge.
- Place the "croissants" on the prepared baking sheet and brush them with the egg wash.
- Bake for 17 to 20 minutes until edges are golden. Drizzle them with the vanilla glaze.

Vanilla Glaze:

1 cup powdered sugar
2 tsp cream
½ tsp clear vanilla extract

Method:

- Mix the glaze ingredients in a small bowl until it is smooth and pourable.
- Drizzle the glaze over the baked "croissants"

Total prep and bake time: 1 hour

Notes & Quotes

Note: *These may also be made into plain biscuits by omitting the filling and simply cutting them into wedges or rounds.*

Banana Bread
Makes: 1 loaf

My daughter and photographer, Katie, requested that I share this recipe. It proved to be popular with many others as well, as it was viewed often on my blog. Fresh warm banana bread is wonderful with melted butter but is just as good with a spread of cream cheese.

1 cup mashed very ripe bananas (about 2 large bananas)

1 cup sugar

½ cup sour cream

¼ cup vegetable oil

2 eggs, lightly beaten

1 ½ cups flour

½ tsp salt

1 tsp baking soda

1 tsp baking powder

Method:

- Preheat oven to 325 °F. Prepare a 9 x 5 inch loaf pan by spraying it with non-stick cooking spray.
- In a large bowl mash the bananas with the white sugar.
- Add the sour cream, eggs and the vegetable oil, just using a large wooden spoon.
- Stir the flour with the salt, baking soda and baking powder.
- Add the mixed flour to the banana mixture.
- Mix just until it is combined. Scoop into prepared loaf pan.
- Bake for 1 hour and 15 minutes.
- Slice and butter it while it is still warm for a wonderful breakfast treat!

Total prep and baking time: 1 ½ hours Photo on chapter title page.

Notes & Quotes

"If you want to make a great friend, go to someone's house and eat with them…the people who give you their food give you their heart."

– Cesa Chavez

Sweet Endings, Sweet Beginnings and Some Sweet Beverages

The dessert recipes I have shared here are some of the best and you can easily make someone very happy with a tray of these favorites. Purchase plenty of disposable containers because they all make wonderful gifts!

Strawberry Meringue Kisses

Makes: 5 dozen

A book could be written about these. The stories would be about how much people love them, stories about how many were eaten in one sitting, sad stories about the guests who didn't get a chance to try them and stories about how many times they are ordered for dessert buffets. They are one bite of "melt in your mouth" bliss. The photo for these is on the chapter header page.

5 dozen prepared meringues (recipe below)
4 oz. cream cheese
2 tbsp. powdered sugar

1 tsp vanilla
⅓ cup whipping cream
1 pint fresh strawberries, washed

Method:

- Slice the strawberries into wedges. Place them in a medium bowl and set them aside.
- Beat the cream cheese with the powdered sugar and vanilla, in a medium size bowl.
- Slowly add the whipping cream until it is smooth.
- Carefully scoop the filling into a small zip lock bag. Make sure it is closed.
- Cut a ¼ inch corner off the edge of the bag.
- Top the meringues by squeezing about 1 tsp of filling on top of the meringue and top it with a strawberry wedge. Place them on a platter.
- Serve immediately.

The Recipe for Meringue Shells:

4 egg whites at room temperature
¾ cup white sugar

Pinch of cream of tartar
1 tsp vanilla extract (preferably clear vanilla)

Method:

- Preheat oven to 225° F. Prepare 2 baking sheets by covering them with parchment paper.
- Beat egg whites at low speed with the cream of tartar for 30 seconds.
- Continue to beat the egg whites at high speed until stiff peaks form.
- Add the sugar, 1 tbsp. at a time waiting at least 15 seconds between each addition. Be mindful to do it slowly as this determines the outcome of the meringues.
- When all the sugar is added, beat in the vanilla extract.
- Pipe or scoop 1 inch mounds or circles of meringue onto the prepared parchment sheets. Use a small spoon to scoop out some of the middle to make a small well for the filling.
- Place them in the preheated oven and bake them for 1 hour. Turn the oven off.

Note: *Meringues can be used in many different recipes. They are supreme with a lemon curd topping, chocolate drizzle or crushed in a whipped cream and fruit parfait.*

Notes & Quotes

- Leave the meringues in the oven and set the timer for another hour, being sure to let others know that the oven is occupied!
- After an hour the meringues should easily peel off the parchment. (This is the fun part!)
- The meringues need to cool slightly before adding any toppings.
- Meringue shells need to be stored in an air tight container at room temperature. They can be stored for up to a week.

Million Dollar Brownies

Million Dollar Brownies are very rich, so they can be sliced in small pieces to frost and decorate. There are so many things you can do with a batch of brownies!
Use a dark thin glaze type frosting, a fluffy frosting with swirls
of chocolate, or serve them warm with ice cream.

¾ cup cocoa
1 cup brown sugar
1 cup white sugar
1 cup melted butter

3 large eggs
1 tsp vanilla
1 cup flour
½ tsp baking powder

Method:

- Preheat oven to 350 °F. Coat a 9 x 13 dish with nonstick cooking spray.
- In a medium bowl, with a wire whisk, stir the sugars with the cocoa. Whisk in the butter until it is smooth, dark and chocolate-y.
- Add the eggs one at a time mixing after each addition. Add the vanilla and whisk well.
- Stir in the flour and baking powder. Chopped nuts can be added at this point if you like.
- The brownie dough will be quite thick. Spread into the greased dish and place in preheated oven for 26 minutes, no longer. Set the timer and run when it rings so you get the right dense, moist and rich chocolate texture! Frosting recipes on page 107.

Total prep and baking time: about 45 minutes
*Recipe credit to: Niece Alanna

Mocha Sponge Cake

This cake (actually called **Mock Sponge Cake**) brings me back to Foods classes in high school and my favorite teacher, Miss van Reeuwyk. Mocha Cake always turned out well for us and we had to use it often to impress other students and teachers. I still use it to impress people.

7 eggs, separated
1 cup sugar
1 tsp vanilla extract

1 cup flour
1 tsp baking powder

Method:

- Preheat the oven to 350° F. Assemble a 9 inch spring form pan. Do not grease the pan.
- Separate the eggs into two bowls. Use a small bowl for the yolks and a large bowl for the whites.
- Use an electric mixer to whip the egg whites. Begin with the mixer on low speed until they are frothy, and then turn up the mixer to high speed. This ensures the most volume.
- When the egg whites form soft peaks, add the sugar slowly, 1 tablespoon at a time. Beat the egg whites until all the sugar is mixed in.
- Add the vanilla extract to the egg yolks and whisk it together with a wire whisk.
- Drizzle the egg yolks into the egg whites with the mixer on low speed.
- Combine the flour with the baking powder and fold it into the egg batter.
- Pour the sponge cake batter into the spring form pan and carefully place it on the middle rack of the oven.
- Bake the cake for 30 to 35 minutes or until the top springs back when pressed on very lightly.
- If possible, prop the cake upside down while it is cooling.

To assemble the Mocha Sponge Cake:

- When the cake has completely cooled, slice it in half.
- Use a long bread knife to slice the cake in half. Place toothpicks around the sides of the cake at the halfway point. Using these as guides, slice the entire circumference of the cake with the knife.
- Set one half aside and apply Quick Pastry Cream (recipe page 106) to the bottom half.
- Carefully place the top half over the pastry cream.
- Use a large flexible metal spatula to apply the **Mocha Cream** (recipe page 106) to the sides and top of the cake.
- Decorate the top of the cake with swirls of melted chocolate.

Chocolate Drizzle:

2 tbsp. semi-sweet chocolate chips
1 tsp vegetable oil

Method:

- Place the chocolate and oil in a heavy duty zip lock bag.
- Float the bag in a bowl of very hot water until the chocolate is melted.
- Snip about ½ cm. off of the bag and use the bag to pipe swirls of chocolate onto the cake.
- Use a toothpick to swirl through for a web effect if you like!

Total prep and baking time: 1 hour, final assembling time; additional hour

Notes & Quotes

Note: Mock Sponge Cake *is an excellent cake to serve with fresh strawberries and whipped cream.*

Apple Crisp
Serves: 10 to 12

Apple Crisp needs no introduction. It has stood the test of time and is always a dependable dessert. Even when I over-bake this and it turns to apple *sauce* crisp, it is devoured!

For the apples:
10 cups Granny Smith apples, peeled and sliced ¾ inch thick
2 tbsp. fresh squeezed lemon juice

For the topping:
1 ½ cups packed light brown sugar
1 ¼ cups all-purpose flour
¾ cups old fashioned oats
½ tsp salt
2 tsp cinnamon
1 cup cold unsalted butter, cut up in small pieces

Method:

- Preheat oven to 375 ° F.
- Layer the apples in a 9 x 13 baking dish. Use more apples if your dish is deep. Sprinkle the lemon juice over the apples.
- In a large bowl, mix the dry ingredients together.
- Add the bits of cut up butter and use an electric mixer to incorporate the dry ingredients with the butter. This is quite messy, so make sure your bowl is big enough. Beat this well, about until the butter comes together with the dry ingredients. The topping should look like very coarse crumbs.
- Carefully crumble the "clumps" over the sliced apples. Lightly press it onto the apples. Make sure you don't flatten it though.
- Bake the Apple Crisp for 15 minutes at 375 ° F and then turn the oven to 350° F and bake for another 40 minutes. The edges should be bubbling a little. If your dish is extra deep give it at least another 15 minutes.
- Serve the apple crisp warm with ice cream.

Total prep and bake time: about 1 ½ hours

Note: *Cold, unsalted butter is crucial for a perfect tender crisp topping.*

Texas Citrus Slice

Yield: about 12 slices

Since oranges and lemons grow so well in the state of Texas, we named a dessert for it. This light dessert is the perfect grand finale after a filling dinner. So many people enjoy this tangy and creamy slice and I am often requested to take it to "gatherings".

Crust:
2 cups graham cracker crumbs
½ cup melted butter
Topping:
1-8 oz. pkg. cream cheese
¼ cup sugar

1-3 oz. box orange flavored gelatin
¾ cup boiling water
¼ cup ice water, (measured with ice)
2 tbsp. fresh squeezed lemon juice
¾ cup whipping cream
1-8 oz. can mandarin orange segments

Method:

- Mix together the crumbs with the melted butter to make the crust.
- Press the graham crumbs into an 8x8 square pan.
- Chill the crust while making the topping.
- Bring some water to a boil; at least a cup.
- Beat the cream until it is stiff and set it in the fridge.
- With an electric mixer on high speed, beat the cream cheese with the sugar in a medium bowl until it is creamy.
- In a separate bowl dissolve the gelatin in the ¾ cup boiling water.
- When the gelatin is completely dissolved, add the ice water and the lemon juice. Stir it well.
- With the mixer going, slowly drizzle the orange gelatin into the cream cheese. Make sure you add it slowly while you are beating it.
- With a wire whisk, add the whipped cream and then fold in the oranges.
- Pour the topping over the chilled base and chill the Texas Citrus slice for about 2 hours or until it is firm.
- Enjoy with a small dollop of whipped cream.

Total prep time: 35 minutes

Notes & Quotes

"I figured if I was going to make the world a better place, I'd do it with cookies."

– Ana Pascal...I bet she did!

Quick "New York Style" Cheesecake

This cheesecake is nice and light, moist, smooth and easy to make. And to give you an idea of how delicious it is...I served a slice to my daughter and told her just to sample it. A couple bites or so, I said. I came back to get the rest and she was viciously scraping the plate, grinning sheepishly! You need to plan ahead for this cheesecake because it does need to chill for about 4 hours to set it completely. It can be made a day or two ahead, though.

Graham Crust:
1 cup graham cracker crumbs
1 tbsp. white sugar
¼ cup melted butter
For the Filling:
2 eggs
⅔ cup sugar

½ cup cottage cheese (2% or 4% is fine)
2 tbsp. cornstarch
1 tbsp. lemon juice
1 tsp vanilla extract
12 oz. cream cheese (1 ½ - 8 oz. pkgs.)
8 oz. sour cream (1 cup)

Method:

- Preheat oven to 325° F. Prepare a 9 inch pie plate by spraying it with non-stick cooking spray, or use an 8 inch spring form pan.
- In a medium size bowl, combine the sugar and graham crumbs. Stir in the melted butter to make a crumbly mixture.
- Press the crumbs, just into the base of the plate. Set base aside to make the filling.
- In a blender or food processor, place the eggs, sugar, cottage cheese, cornstarch, lemon juice and vanilla.
- Cover and blend at medium speed for 1 minute. Cut up the cream cheese into about 10 chunks.
- Add the cream cheese one chunk at a time, blending until it is smooth.
- Stop your blender or food processor, and add the sour cream.
- Blend in the sour cream briefly, about 10 seconds, just until it is smooth.
- Pour the creamy filling into the graham crust and place in the oven.
- Bake for 35 to 40 minutes or until the filling is set around the edge. (When you touch it lightly in the middle, it won't jiggle)
- Cool for about an hour on a cooling rack before chilling it completely in the refrigerator.
- Serve with chilled strawberry sauce or any of your favorite toppings.

Total prep and bake time: 45 minutes

Dreamy Chocolate Mousse Cupcakes
Makes: 18 cupcakes

Oh for the love of chocolate...

Chocolate Cupcakes:
1 cup flour
¾ cup sugar
⅓ cup cocoa powder
¾ tsp baking powder
1 tsp baking soda

½ tsp salt
½ cup milk
½ cup coffee
⅓ vegetable oil
1 egg
1 tsp vanilla extract

Method:

- Preheat oven to 350° F. Line 18 muffin tins with paper liners.
- Mix the dry ingredients in a medium size bowl and whisk them together well.
- In a separate bowl whisk together the liquid ingredients.
- Using the wire whisk, stir in the liquid ingredients. Whisk it together until there are no lumps in the batter.
- Fill the muffin cups about ¾ full.
- Bake the cupcakes for about 18 minutes or until the tops spring back when lightly touched.
- Cool completely before filling them with **Chocolate Mousse**. (recipe and assembly directions on page 88)

Boterkoek! Dutch Butter Cake
Makes: 2 pie shaped Koeken

Just like Oma used to make! Many of my Dutch friends and relatives will probably recognize this recipe and they have probably made it often as well. It brings back childhood memories of afternoons at Oma and Opa's house (Grandma and Grandpa) and all the love it was made with. This recipe is easy but there are a few things that make it just right. The oven time and the type of dish you bake it in definitely make all the difference. You want the edges to be crunchy and the middle to be moist and dense. I have the best success when I use disposable aluminum pie plates. I'm not sure why this gives the best textured Boterkoek but it really does. Probably some science involved here again!

1 ½ cups butter, soft
2 cups sugar
1 tbsp. pure almond extract
2 eggs

3 cups flour
1 tsp baking powder
(Cream and sliced almonds for topping)

Method:

- Preheat the oven to 325° F. Prepare 2 aluminum pie plates (disposable type) by spraying them with non-stick cooking spray.
- Measure the butter into a large bowl and beat with an electric mixer until smooth.
- Add the sugar and beat just until combined.
- Crack both of the eggs into the bowl and also add the almond extract. Beat to incorporate it well.
- Stir the flour with the baking powder and then add it to the creamed mixture. Beat until the batter is stiff and the flour is completely mixed in.
- Scoop the dough into the two pans, dividing it evenly, spreading it in with slightly wet hand.
- Brush the top with a little cream to make it smooth and so it bakes up nice and shiny. You could also top it with some sliced almonds if you like.
- Bake at 325 for 40 minutes and no longer. (Glass plates will bake the **Boterkoek** quicker)
- Let the cakes cool before popping them out of the tins and cutting them into nice long triangle slices.

Total prep and bake time: about 1 hour

Note: *This Dutch Butter Cake recipe or Boterkoek, is the top searched recipe on my website. I am pretty sure I have a strong Dutch following!*

Notes & Quotes

Chocolate Mousse

1 pkg. unflavored gelatin
3 tbsp. cold water
¼ cup boiling water
3 oz. semi sweet baking chocolate

¼ cup powdered sugar
1 tsp vanilla extract
1 ½ cups whipping cream

Method:

- In a medium size bowl pour the cold water over the gelatin. Set the bowl aside to soften for 2 minutes.
- Add the boiling water to the softened gelatin and stir it until the gelatin is dissolved. At this point divide the melted gelatin in *half*. Discard the other half.
- Place the chocolate in a heavy duty zip lock bag and dip it in very hot water until it is melted. Whisk the melted chocolate into the warm dissolved gelatin.
- Use an electric mixer to whip the cream with the powdered sugar and vanilla until it is stiff.
- Carefully fold in the melted chocolate and gelatin mixture, being careful to keep the volume of the whipped cream.
- Scoop the mousse into a large heavy duty zip lock bag. Chill it until you are ready to use it.
- To assemble cupcakes from page 85: Cut a cone shape piece out of each of the cupcakes.
- Pipe a swirl of mousse into the cupcake, filling it nice and full.
- Use a piece of the cake top as a decoration for the top of the cupcake.
- Dust the cupcakes with a little sifted powdered sugar before serving them.
- Enjoy the dreamy expressions on your friends and families faces!

Total prep, baking and assembling time for chocolate mousse cupcakes: 1 ½ hours maximum

Note: *The cupcake and mousse recipe may be doubled to make* **Chocolate Mousse Cake**. *Top it with vanilla whipped cream and chocolate curls for a wonderful dessert.*

Pina Colada Mousse
Makes: about 6 small servings

Exotic, creamy and impressive enough to serve to the most distinguished guests. Upon sharing this recipe with my cooking class, I received many recipe requests. It really is quite simple to make!

Melt together:
16 large marshmallows
⅓ cup pineapple juice
Add:
1 tsp fresh squeezed lemon juice

¼ cup pineapple juice
½ tsp coconut extract
Whip:
½ cup whipping cream

Method:

- In a medium saucepan melt the marshmallows with the pineapple juice until the mixture is smooth. Remove from the heat.
- Whisk in the lemon juice, the additional ¼ cup of pineapple juice and the coconut extract. Chill for about half hour in the freezer, stirring occasionally.
- Whip the cream in a medium bowl until it is stiff. Reserve 2 tbsp. for topping the finished mousse.
- Fold the cooled pineapple juice and marshmallows mixture into the whipped cream.
- Pipe or scoop the mousse into about 6 small cups (¼ cup each). Top each small cup with a small swirl of whipped cream and chill them* for about 1 hour.

Total prep and chill time: 1 hour
*the mousse may be frozen briefly to speed up the setting process.

Mom's Butter Tarts
Makes: about 2 dozen

If there is one treat that I can't resist, it has got to be **Butter tarts**. I remember when my sister and I used to sneak them out of the basement freezer and eat them frozen! I'm sure my mom wondered why they disappeared so quickly! Once we learned to make them ourselves they didn't even make it to the freezer! Butter tarts are just right when the crust is crumbly and the filling just about oozes out when you bite into it. Mom's Butter Tarts are all that!

Pastry Dough:
2 ½ cups flour
6 tbsp. powdered sugar
1 ⅓ cup soft butter
Filling:
3 eggs

1 cup corn syrup
⅔ cup packed brown sugar
⅓ cup melted butter
1 tsp vanilla
⅛ tsp salt
1 cup raisins (optional)

Method:

- Preheat oven to 375° F. Use 2 regular size muffin tins or 24 tart tins.
- Combine the flour and powdered sugar in a large bowl.
- Cut in or use an electric mixer on low speed to combine the butter with the flour. Mix together until the mixture is crumbly.
- Divide the dough among 22 to 24 muffin cups or fluted metal tart tins.
- Press the dough evenly over the bottom and up the sides of the tins.
- Sprinkle raisins over the bottoms of each tin if desired. Prepare the filling.

Filling:

- In a medium size bowl whisk together the eggs, corn syrup, brown sugar, melted butter, vanilla and salt.
- Pour into the tart shells, being careful not to drip or over fill. The tarts can be filled to about 2 cm. from the top edge of the crust.
- Bake for about 20 to 25 minutes or until the filling is almost set. The edges will be golden. Cool at least 10 minutes before removing them from the pans.

Total prep and baking time: 1 hour

Notes & Quotes

Note: *The filling may be prepared and frozen. Thaw the filling in the refrigerator and stir it before use.*

Chocolate Kahlua Truffle Tarts

Makes: 24 tarts

These tarts have a filling that resembles a smooth and creamy truffle. The whipped cream topping infused with more Kahlua gives these tarts a beautiful flavor and presentation. With a name like this one, you'll want to label your dessert tray!

Use 24 pre-baked tart shells that have been cooled.

Kahlua Truffle Tarts Filling:

Stir together:

⅓ cup white sugar

2 tbsp. cornstarch

⅛ tsp salt

Whisk in:

½ cup milk

½ cup cream (half and half)

3 egg yolks, lightly beaten

Add:

1 tsp vanilla extract

1 tbsp. butter

¼ cup Kahlua

4 oz. semi-sweet chocolate

Method:

- In a medium size saucepan stir together the cornstarch with the sugar and the salt. (Do not turn on the heat yet.)
- Pour in the milk and cream and whisk it into the cornstarch mixture. Whisk in the egg yolks as well.
- Set the stove on medium heat and stir the creamy filling constantly using a wire whisk.
- Continue cooking until the filling just comes to a boil. Turn the filling to low and continue to stir well for about 30 more seconds.
- Remove the filling from the heat and add the vanilla, butter, Kahlua and the semi-sweet chocolate. Stir until it is very smooth.
- Pour or scoop the Chocolate Kahlua Truffle Filling into the baked tart shells. Fill them ⅔ full. There should be exactly enough filling to fill 24 tarts.
- Cover the tarts lightly with waxed paper and chill them while preparing the whipped cream topping.

The Recipe for the Whipped Cream Topping:

1 ½ cups whipping cream

3 tbsp. powdered sugar

1 tsp vanilla extract

2 to 3 tbsp. Kahlua

Method:

- Whip the whipping cream with an electric mixer until it is fluffy but not stiff.
- Add the powdered sugar, vanilla and the Kahlua and beat until it is firm.
- Place the whipped cream in a bag with a star tip to pipe it on top of the cooled, filled tarts.

Chocolate Curls and Chocolate Hearts

Chocolate curls and chocolate hearts are easy to make! For the curls, hold a block of chocolate in your hand and use a vegetable peeler or cheese slicer to make curls or shaved chocolate. The longer you hold the chocolate in your hand the more the chocolate curls!

For the hearts, melt 1 oz. of semi-sweet chocolate in a heavy duty zip lock bag in a bowl of very hot water. When the chocolate is melted snip a ¼ cm corner off the tip and pipe hearts onto wax paper. Freeze the hearts until they are firm and peel them off the wax paper to use them as pretty accents for your tarts!

Total prep and cook time: about 45 minutes

Glazed Almond Turnovers

Makes: 1 dozen large or 2 dozen mini Turnovers

Flaky pastry, rich almond filling and the decorative glaze makes these Glazed Almond Turnovers very impressive. They are quite often the first item to disappear on my dessert platters. Using frozen purchased puff pastry cuts the prep time for these, but don't be afraid to try your hand at homemade puff pastry; the results are worth it!

1 package frozen puff pastry, thawed or homemade (Page 105)

Egg wash:
1 egg
1 tbsp. water

Almond Filling:
1 pound almond paste
1 ½ cups sugar
½ cup flour
3 eggs
1 tbsp. lemon juice
½ tsp almond extract

Method:

- Preheat oven to 400° F. Prepare a baking sheet by covering it with parchment paper.
- Whisk the egg and water together in a small bowl to make the egg wash. Set this aside.
- To make the almond filling grate the almond paste into a large bowl.
- Add the sugar and flour and stir it together with a fork.
- Use an electric mixer to mix in the eggs, lemon juice and the almond extract. The dough will be very stiff.
- On a lightly floured surface, roll out each of the puff pastry sheets so that it is one and a half times the size of the original slab, or to about 1 cm. thick.
- Cut out the pastry into 3 by 3 inch squares, for large turnovers, or 1 ½ by 1 ½ for mini turnovers. (Using a pizza cutter for this is very effective.)
- Place about 2 tbsp. of almond filling on one side of the pastry square. (1 tbsp. for the mini's)
- Brush a little egg wash all along the edge of the pastry square. Carefully fold the pastry over to make a triangle, lining up the edges. Do not stretch the pastry as it will shrink back and break the seal.
- Press the edges down with a fork. Make sure they are sealed.
- Place the turnovers on the prepared baking sheet and brush the tops with egg wash.
- Make a few small slashes on the tops of the pastry with a small knife to allow steam to escape.
- Bake the turnovers for about 20 to 22 minutes or until they are golden and crispy. Let them cool slightly before drizzling them lightly with the glaze.

Glaze:

1 cup powdered sugar
1 to 2 tbsp. cream

½ tsp clear vanilla extract
¼ tsp almond extract

Method:

- Mix together the glaze in a small bowl, adding extra cream as needed to make a glaze the consistency of thick syrup.
- Lightly drizzle over the almond turnovers.

Total prep and bake time: about 1 hour

Oatmeal Pecan Lace Cookies

Makes: 24 cookies; 12 filled

These Oatmeal Pecan Lace Cookies are scrumptious just the way they
are but become truly amazing with the Mocha Cream Filling.

Oatmeal and Pecan Lace Cookies:
½ cup unsalted soft butter
¾ cup packed brown sugar
2 tbsp. flour*
¼ tsp salt

2 tbsp. milk
1 tsp vanilla extract
1 ¼ cups rolled oats (not quick cooking)
¼ cup finely chopped pecans
Mocha Cream (about ⅓ recipe) recipe page 106

Method:

- Preheat oven to 350 degrees. Prepare 4 baking sheets by covering them with parchment paper.
- Beat the butter with the sugar until it is light and fluffy, about 3 minutes.
- Add the milk, flour and salt all at once and beat for about 30 seconds.
- Stir in the vanilla extract and then stir in the oats and chopped pecans.
- Roll the dough into smaller than an inch size balls. You will have very greasy hands. Good time for the phone to ring!
- Place them on the prepared baking sheets about 3 inches apart. Don't be tempted to put them closer together! They spread out to be very thin and will spread into each other if they are too close.
- Bake them for about 12 minutes or until they are a nice brown color. They need to be quite brown to get the crispiness you are trying to achieve. Bake only one tray at a time.
- Let them rest on the baking sheet for at least 5 minutes before removing them to completely cool on a flat surface. These cookies are delicate and need to be handled carefully. Fill them when they are cool.

*Don't be confused about the flour amount on this recipe. Two tablespoons of flour is not a typo! They need to spread out.

Mocha Filled Lace Cookies Directions

To use the Mocha Butter Cream for a filling for the Oatmeal Pecan Lace Cookies, scoop the mocha cream into a heavy duty zip lock bag. Snip a ¼ inch off of one corner of the bag to use it to pipe onto the cookie. (Piping the frosting onto the cookie works better than spreading it on because the cookies are very fragile.) Pipe about 4 strips of mocha cream onto each cookie before topping it with the other cookie. Make sure you have the textured sides up on the cookies. Lay the filled Oatmeal Pecan Lace Cookies flat on a wax paper covered baking sheet. Chill until they are firm. Mocha filled Lace cookies will last about 3 days in the refrigerator in a sealed container and only if they are hidden.

Total bake and prep time: 1 hour

Glazed Mixed Nuts

Makes: about 3 cups

Nothing says "I love you" more than something homemade! **Glazed Mixed Nuts** are just what you need for a quick and special gift. They are crispy, slightly sweet and very satisfying. I use almonds and pecans but you can use whatever nuts you'd like. The cute cone shape container is easy to make and I've included instructions for it.

2 pounds unsalted mixed nuts
4 tbsp. melted butter
¼ cup packed brown sugar
¼ cup light corn syrup

½ tsp salt
1 tsp vanilla extract
½ to 1 tsp cinnamon

Method:

- Preheat oven to 350° F. Prepare a baking sheet by coating it heavily with non-stick cooking spray.
- Mix the melted butter with the brown sugar, corn syrup, salt, vanilla and the cinnamon in a large bowl. Stir it well with a whisk to make thick syrup.
- Stir in the nuts to coat them well with the syrup.
- Spread the nuts out onto the prepared baking sheet and drizzle any remaining syrup over them.
- Bake the nuts for 20 minutes. Stir them every 5 minutes while they are baking to get an even coating. They will bubble in the oven and the butter seems to separate, but don't worry, they turn out at the end!
- After they come out of the oven toss them around in the syrup to get the coating to stick on them. The nuts take about 10 minutes to cool and crisp up. Break apart the clumps.
- Cool them completely before packaging them.

Total prep and bake time: 1 hour

To make the cone shape container:

1. Cut out a 7 by 7 square out of card stock paper that has been printed on both sides.
2. Fold the paper to make a cone shape by sliding the side corners together.
3. Tape or glue the edges down to secure the cone.
4. Make a bend in the point of the cone to make a "lid".
5. You may line the cone with wax paper to keep the cone from getting greasy.
6. Add the Glazed Mixed Nuts and you have the cutest homemade food gift ever!

New Jersey Ice Box Cupcakes

Makes: 5 large cupcakes

Ice Box Cake recipes are usually from pretty old cookbooks. When studying the state of New Jersey in a cooking class, Ice Box Cake was found to be originated there. The original Ice Box Cake was actually a white cake made from scratch, which had several layers and a topping of fresh whipped cream. Since this cake was made before the days of refrigeration, it had to be cooled for at least 24 hours over blocks of ice, and thus considered quite extravagant! These cupcakes are just as extravagant but only take a fraction of the preparation time!

20 chocolate wafers (Nabisco Brand is good)
1 ½ cups whipping cream
3 tbsp. powdered sugar

1 tsp clear vanilla extract
¼ cup chocolate curls (about 2 oz. semi-sweet chocolate)

Method:

- Set aside 20 chocolate wafers.
- Whip the cream in a large bowl with an electric mixer or with a whisk.
- Add the powdered sugar and the vanilla extract and mix until the whipping cream is firm but not overly stiff.
- Put the whip cream into a heavy duty gallon size zip lock bag. Snip off a ¼ inch corner.
- Squeeze out a big circle of whipped cream onto 5 wafers.
- Continue topping the cream and layering the wafers until they are all stacked, using 4 wafers for each stack.
- Now cover each cupcake stack with whipped cream. Begin making the chocolate curls.*
- Use wax paper to pour the chocolate curls over the cupcakes.
- Place your beautiful creations into the refrigerator in a covered container. Make sure the lid does not touch the cupcakes. Chill for at least 6 hours.
- Slice your New Jersey Ice Box Cupcakes in half to serve them and show off all the wonderful layers.
- Total prep time: 20 minutes (not including chilling time)

*Directions for chocolate curls are with the Chocolate Kahlua Tart recipe.

Indiana Caramel Corn

Makes: 8 cups caramel corn

Whether you package Indiana Caramel Corn in pretty bags for gifts or use it for a family snack, this crispy caramel corn is irresistible. Since Indiana grows the most corn for popping in all of the United States, we thought it necessary to name this caramel corn for it. Prepare to get requests for this as soon as you sit down to relax in the evening!

8 cups popped corn
¾ cups packed brown sugar
⅓ cup butter
3 tbsp. corn syrup

¼ tsp baking soda
½ tsp vanilla
¼ tsp to ½ tsp salt

Method:

- Preheat oven to 300° F.
- After popping the corn, place it on a heavily greased baking tray. Remove any un-popped kernels.
- Spray a medium size saucepan with non-stick cooking spray.
- In the saucepan, place the sugar, butter and corn syrup.
- Cook and stir on medium heat until the mixture comes to a boil. Turn the heat lower and continue to cook and stir while the mixture is at a low boil. Stir gently, this gets extremely hot.
- Keep stirring while it is at a low boil for about 8 minutes. Check the caramel every 2 minutes to see if it is at hard ball* stage. When the caramel is at the hard ball stage remove it from the heat.

- Add the soda and vanilla extract and stir it briskly.
- Pour the hot caramel over the popped corn on the baking sheet. Gently stir it to coat the popcorn a little. Make sure you have an even layer of popcorn on the tray. Lightly salt the popcorn on the tray.
- Bake the popcorn for about 20 minutes, stirring it every 5 minutes. Make sure you take the tray out of the oven to stir it, because it can become a little messy. The Caramel corn is done when the caramel is crispy.
- Let the caramel corn rest on the tray for at least 10 minutes before serving it.

Total prep and baking time: about 45 minutes
*To test candy stages, fill a bowl with cold water. When you drip a little caramel in the cold water, it will turn hard and brittle if it is at the "hard ball" stage.

Almond Triangles
Makes: about 48 triangles

I'm so excited about this recipe! I have been trying to make the perfect almond slice but so many have turned out either too dry or too sticky. *Then*, I created this recipe! These Almond Triangles turned out just the way I wanted them to. They are so quick and easy to make; the only thing that takes time is waiting for them to cool before slicing and eating them.

Base:
1 ½ cups flour
½ cup packed brown sugar
¼ tsp salt
½ tsp almond extract
½ cup butter

Almond Topping:
2 ½ cups sliced almonds
1 cup white chocolate chips
2 tbsp. butter
½ cup corn syrup
¾ tsp almond extract
¼ tsp salt

Method:

- Preheat oven to 350°F. Use a 9 x 13 ungreased baking dish.
- Place the flour, sugar and salt in the bowl of a food processor. Pulse the food processor for a few seconds to blend.
- Cut up the butter into about 6 pieces and place it in the food processor with the flour mixture. Blend this together for about 30 seconds or until the mixture resembles fine crumbs.
- Pour the crumbs into the 9x13 baking dish and press the base in firmly.
- Bake for 10 minutes.
- Prepare the almond topping while the base is baking.

Almond Topping:

- Measure out the 2 ½ cups almonds. Set these aside.
- In a heavy duty saucepan melt the white chocolate chips with the butter and the corn syrup. Keep the heat on very low and stir until the butter and chips are melted.
- Stir in the almond extract and the salt.
- Sprinkle the almonds evenly over the baked crust.
- Pour the melted white chocolate mixture over the sliced almonds, careful to evenly distribute it. It will spread as it bakes so don't fret over it too much!
- Return the baking dish to the oven and bake 15 minutes more until the almonds glaze over and become beautifully golden.
- Cool completely before slicing into triangles.

Total prep and baking time: 35 minutes

Note: *These amazing **Almond Triangles** last for several days in an air tight container at room temperature. They can also be frozen for up to 2 months.*

Rocky Road Candy Bars

Makes: about 16 bars

Salted pretzels make these Rocky Road Bars unique and very hard to resist. When I start eating these, I tell myself that marshmallows are basically just air and thus these bars are *practically* diet food! Little kids and very big kids finish these bars off in no time!

1 cup semi-sweet chocolate chips
1 cup milk chocolate chips
¼ cup smooth peanut butter

2 tbsp. butter
2 cups miniature marshmallows
1 ½ cups coarsely chopped pretzels

Method:

- In a heavy saucepan on very low heat, melt the chocolate, peanut butter and the butter. Stir it gently as it melts.
- Let the chocolate rest for 10 minutes to let it cool down.
- Meanwhile prepare an 8x8 square dish by lining it with foil and spraying it with non-stick cooking spray.
- Add the pretzels and marshmallows to the melted chocolate.
- Spread the Rocky Road into the prepared dish. Chill for at least 2 hours before cutting them into squares.

Total prep and cooking time: about 20 minutes not including setting time

Quick Puff Pastry
Makes: 1 ½ pounds pastry dough

Homemade puff pastry is by far the best tasting puff pastry. There is a great amount of satisfaction in completing this recipe. If you master this, well, the possibilities are endless! You have all sorts of amazing desserts and appetizers at your fingertips and that for a fraction of the price of store-bought pastry! Don't be daunted by the extensive directions, you will be glad they are there for you. Once you make this, you will be so excited and want to brag about it to everyone! And everyone will smile at you and tell you you're amazing...

1 ¼ cups cold unsalted butter (2 ½ sticks)
½ cup very cold water

1 tsp salt
2 cups flour

Method:

- Cut up 1 cup of the cold butter into ¼ inch size pieces and place it on a plate to chill in the refrigerator while you prepare the remaining ingredients.
- Stir the salt into the cold water to dissolve it and set it aside.
- Place the 2 cups of flour into the bowl of a food processor fitted with a metal blade.
- Dice the remaining ¼ cup of butter very small and place it in the food processor. Make sure it is cold.
- Pulse the food processor twelve times using one second pulses. The mixture should be crumbly but not powder.
- Add the remaining 1 cup chopped, cold butter and pulse another 5 times.
- Pour in the water and pulse about 4 more times or until the dough comes together just a little. Do not over process, bits of butter will still be visible.
- Place a 2 foot long piece of plastic wrap on your countertop. Have another the same size ready. Dust the plastic wrap with a little flour.
- Shape the pastry dough into a rough rectangle shape and place it on the plastic wrap. Cover it with the other piece of plastic and work it with your hands to make it stick together a little.
- Use a rolling pin to flatten it to about 1 inch thick. Don't worry about the crumbles and rough edges, you can tuck them in later.
- Remove the top layer of plastic wrap and fold the slab in thirds, accordion style.
- Press that flat a little and fold that whole slab in half again, length-wise, creating many layers. The butter will show in the layers.
- Chill the pastry for at least an hour or for up to 4 days, covered well.
- Rolled out pastry bakes at 400 degrees for 20 minutes or as directed in recipe.

Total prep time: 40 minutes

Notes & Quotes

Note: *Puff pastry may be frozen and thawed in the refrigerator when needed.*

Quick Pastry Cream Filling
Makes: 2 cups

The amazing Mocha Sponge Cake Filling!

8 oz. softened cream cheese
¼ cup sugar
1 tsp clear vanilla extract

¾ cup milk
2 oz. instant vanilla pudding
1 cup whipping cream

Method:

- In a medium size bowl whip the cream until it is firm but not stiff. Set the bowl aside.
- Beat the cream cheese, sugar and vanilla with an electric mixer until it is light and fluffy.
- Add the milk in a slow drizzle, while continuing to mix.
- Pour in the pudding mix and beat the filling until it is smooth and thick.
- Fold the whipped cream into the creamy vanilla mixture.
- Use the Pastry Cream Filling to fill the **Mocha Sponge Cake** from page 80.

Total prep time: 15 minutes

Mocha Butter Cream
Makes: about 2 ½ cups cream

Most butter cream frosting or filling recipes require using a cooked syrup. This recipe is a "sped up" version. The same silky texture is achieved because of the use of hot instant espresso. Mocha Butter Cream can be used as a filling for the Oatmeal Pecan Lace Cookies but it is also perfect to frost the Mocha Sponge Cake.

1 ½ cup butter
3 tbsp. instant espresso or coffee granules
6 tbsp. hot coffee

2 tsp pure vanilla extract
1 ½ cups powdered sugar, sifted

Method:

- In a medium size mixing bowl beat the butter with an electric mixer until it is light and fluffy.
- Stir the espresso granules with the hot coffee in a small bowl.
- Pour one tablespoon of the hot coffee into the whipped butter. Beat well.
- Sprinkle half of the powdered sugar over the butter mixture and beat well.
- Add the vanilla extract and the remaining coffee and beat until smooth.
- Beat in the remaining powdered sugar and test it to make sure it is smooth and creamy.

Total prep time: about 10 minutes

Rich Chocolate Frosting

This Rich chocolate Frosting is the best option for a dark, glaze type frosting for your **Million Dollar Brownies.**

½ cup very soft butter, not melted though
⅔ cup cocoa powder
1 cup powdered sugar

2 tbsp. cream or milk
2 tbsp. hot coffee
1 tbsp. vanilla extract

Method:

- Place all the ingredients in a medium size bowl and whisk briskly to make a smooth and silky frosting. Spread onto the chilled brownies.
- This is a relatively thin layer of frosting but it can be doubled if you prefer it thicker.

Fluffy Chocolate Frosting

To make Fluffy Chocolate Frosting that can be piped onto small brownie squares, simply add 1 cup more powdered sugar to the Rich Chocolate frosting. This method, however, requires an electric mixer. Beat all the ingredients until it becomes airy and fluffy. Drizzle 3 types of melted chocolate over the swirled, piped frosting as pictured on the brownies on page 79 or simply spread over the cooled brownies as pictured below.

"Friendly" Fresh Strawberry Margarita

Makes 4 to 6 beverages

A little taste of summer!

2 cups sliced fresh strawberries
½ cup frozen limeade concentrate

2 tbsp. sugar
2 cups ice cubes

Method:

- Simply blend all the ingredients in a blender until they are very smooth.
- Pour into 4 to 6 of your special lime juice and sugar dipped* glasses. Serve immediately.

Note: To make a sugary rim on your glasses, pour some fresh lime juice on one saucer and some sugar onto another saucer. Dip the inverted glasses in the lime juice and then immediately in the sugar. You can make this into an adult beverage by adding Tequila.

Notes & Quotes

Pina Coladas
Yield: 4 to 6 servings

This drink is certain to get some "wows" from your family and friends!

2 cups pineapple juice, cold
½ cup cream of coconut or coconut milk
2 tbsp. sugar
½ cup cold milk

1 ½ cups crushed ice
¼ to ½ tsp coconut extract
2 cups ice cream

Method:

- Place all ingredients in a blender. Make sure the ingredients are all very cold or frozen. (Be careful not to overdo it with the coconut extract!)
- Blend at high speed until very smooth.
- Garnish the Pina Coladas with fresh whipped cream. (The drizzle pictured over the whipped cream, is actually thick pineapple juice.)
- Serve immediately, or freeze it partially and blend it again when you are ready to serve it.

Raspberry Colada Slushy Punch

Serves: about 30

I love serving this punch at parties and showers! Guests find the exotic slushy punch fun and exciting! The Pina Colodas mix keeps the mixture from freezing solid and makes a delicious slush. This has a great "wow" factor.

10 cups Raspberry Cranberry juice
32 oz. bottle Pina Colodas mix

½ cup Raspberry Syrup
64 oz. Ginger Ale

Method:

- Freeze the raspberry juice, Pina colada mix and the syrup in 2 large zip lock bags, overnight.
- Take the frozen punch out of the freezer 30 minutes before making the punch.
- Squish the bag around a little to break up the block and squeeze it out into a punch bowl.
- Slowly add the ginger ale and stir it carefully.
- Serve in short cups with colorful, small fat straws.

Notes & Quotes

Note: *Add a hint of coconut liqueur to serve this your adult guests.*

Homemade Raspberry or Blackberry Syrup:

2 cups fresh raspberries or Blackberries
1 cup sugar
2 cups water

Add:
1 tbsp. lemon juice

Method:

- In a medium saucepan, cook the raspberries or blackberries with the sugar and the water.
- Bring the syrup to a rolling boil and boil it for 2 minutes.
- Remove the raspberry or blackberry syrup from the heat and add the lemon juice. (This helps keep the color bright)
- Strain the syrup through a fine strainer to get a clear syrup.
- Chill or freeze the syrup.

Sparkling Raspberry or Blackberry Lemonade Punch

Yield: Twenty 8 oz. servings or forty 4 oz. servings.

Raspberry Lemonade uses a wonderful homemade Raspberry Syrup that may be frozen and reserved for many other recipes. This Sparkling Raspberry Lemonade was served at a recent event that I catered and it disappeared quickly on that warm summer evening! This punch is just as delicious with blackberries.

¾ cup fresh raspberry or blackberry syrup (recipe follows)
¾ cup purchased raspberry or blackberry syrup
18 oz. (1 ½ cans) frozen lemonade concentrate

1 64 oz. bottle lemon lime soda
1 64 oz. sparkling water or club soda
Ice, lemon slices and raspberries/blackberries for garnish

Method:

- Stir together the lemonade and the raspberry or blackberry syrups in a large punch bowl or beverage dispenser. (Use all homemade blackberry syrup if you can't purchase the prepared kind.)
- Add the lemon lime soda and then some of the ice.
- Stir the punch gently and then add the remaining soda.
- Top with plenty of ice, some lemon slices and raspberries/blackberries.

Mediterranean Sunset

Yield: 6 cups

This fresh, sparkling drink is always a huge hit with my high school cooking classes. It is fun and easy to make and provides you with a good dose of Vitamin C. Just make sure you stir in the soda *after* the strawberries and juices are blended! We have experienced enough volcano type incidents to know that that is definitely the better way! Since all these ingredients are available year round, it is good any time of the year!

2 cups frozen unsweetened strawberries
2 tbsp. fresh squeezed lime juice
4 tbsp. white sugar

2 tbsp. frozen concentrate orange juice
3 cups sparkling water or club soda

Method

- Blend the first 4 ingredients on high speed in a blender.
- Gently stir in the soda or sparkling water.
- Garnish with strawberry halves and lime slices. Serve immediately.
- This recipe makes about 6 cups or fills about 5 goblets. Enjoy!

Sparkling White Grape Punch

Serves: about 20

Especially light and refreshing and excellent to replace white wine.

8 cups white grape juice
1-2 liter bottle of Ginger Ale

4 cups crushed ice

Method:

Pour contents in a punch bowl. Serve immediately.

Twelve Hot Mochas

Cool weather calls for warm drinks. When you need to serve your guests something hot, this larger recipe for mochas is handy to have. It is easy to keep warm on the stove to have ready to pour when your guests arrive. The ice cream topping creates a rich creamy cap.

3 tbsp. instant espresso granules
3 tbsp. boiling water
1 cup chocolate syrup
2 tsp vanilla extract

⅛ tsp salt
9 cups milk, boiled
12 small scoops vanilla ice cream
Chocolate sauce for "drizzle"

Method:

- Bring the milk to a boil.
- In a large pitcher, dissolve the coffee in the boiled water. Stir until dissolved.
- Add the chocolate syrup, salt and the vanilla extract and stir into the coffee mixture.
- Pour the hot milk into the pitcher and stir well. Add more milk to taste. The mochas can be kept warm on the stove in a saucepan at this point.
- Pour into pretty "prepared" coffee cups.
- Add a scoop of ice cream into each cup.
- Drizzle a little bit of chocolate sauce over each beverage.
- Serve the Mocha's when the ice cream has melted slightly.

Total prep and cooking time: 20 minutes

Notes & Quotes

Note: *To give your glass mugs a sparkling sugary rim, dip them first in cold water and then into a layer of sugar.*

Conclusion and Thanks

What an adventure this cook book has been! There are so many wonderful people that I want to thank who contributed so much.

First of all my dear husband, Ken, who has encouraged me so much, coaxed me and given me the confidence I needed to persevere. Thank you so much, Lovey!

All my sons and daughters were so patient with me, serving me coffee when I needed it and often filling my role.

-Thanks, Josh, for your advice and for promoting my website!

-Thanks, Lyssa, for making me feel like a special Mom!

-Thanks, Rachael, for being an awesome sounding board when I was frustrated!

-Thanks, Katie, for stopping everything to take so many photos for me!

-Thanks, Amy, for trying out new recipes for us!

-Thanks, Jared, for making me coffee and for telling me I'm a good cook!

A special thanks to Mom and Papa and Mom and Dad H for enjoying my cooking, encouraging me and giving me opportunities!

Thanks to my sisters and brothers, all of them, for all their support. Julaine, Cheryl and Ruth for your editing and advising, thank you so much!

Thank you to all my cooking class students and fellow workshop teachers at LA! You are all so special to me, I appreciate your smiles and encouragement.

I want to thank Breanna Randall and my niece Beyond, for taking pictures of me and for me and for being so sweet about it!

This cookbook adventure has taught me so much! I certainly could not have done it without the help of so many special friends. And from the Liferich publishing team, with a special thanks to Heather Carter who understood how new every tiny little step was for me and who remained patient with me.

But most of all, thanks goes to the Lord who gives us the gifts to share and who answers prayer.

Contact me at suchgreatrecipes.com